SWIFT AND BEAUTIFUL

The Amazing Stories of Faithful Missionaries

"Take my feet, and let them be
Swift and beautiful for thee."
—Frances Ridley Havergal

David B. Calhoun

THE BANNER OF TRUTH TRUST

THE BANNER OF TRUTH TRUST

Head Office
3 Murrayfield Road
Edinburgh, EH12 6EL
UK

North America Office
PO Box 621
Carlisle, PA 17013
USA

banneroftruth.org

First published 2020
© David B. Calhoun 2020

*

ISBN
Print: 978 1 84871 938 5
EPUB: 978 1 84871 941 5
Kindle: 978 1 84871 964 4

*

Typeset in 10/13 Minion Pro at
The Banner of Truth Trust, Edinburgh

Printed in the USA by
Versa Press Inc.,
East Peoria, IL.

Dedicated with gratitude
to
Wayne Sparkman

Director of the Historical Center
of
The Presbyterian Church in America.

A faithful Christian
A loyal churchman
A devoted husband and father
A competent historian
A skillful archivist
A friend and brother in Christ

CONTENTS

FOREWORD

*"How beautiful are the feet of those who
bring good news"* (Romans 10:15).

ISAIAH the prophet wrote about good news that had come to Israel. "How beautiful upon the mountains are the feet of him who brings good news, who publishes peace, who brings good news of happiness, who publishes salvation, who says to Zion, 'Your God reigns!'" (Isaiah 52:7).[1] The good news that the prophet celebrated was that the people of Israel would return from exile. No doubt Isaiah was also looking ahead to the far greater good news that was coming for all people.

In Romans 10:13 the apostle Paul, quoting Joel 2:32, writes that "everyone who calls on the name of the Lord will be saved." Paul asks some questions. "But how are they to call on him in whom they have not believed? And how are they to believe in him of whom they have never heard? And how are they to hear without someone preaching? And how are they to preach unless they are sent?" Paul adds, quoting

---

[1] The scripture quotations in this section are from the Holy Bible, English Standard Version, copyright © 2001 by Crossway Bibles, a publishing ministry of Good News Publishers. Used by permission. All rights reserved..

the words of Isaiah 52:7, "As it is written, 'How beautiful are the feet of those who preach the good news.'" The gospel, God's good news, is for "all nations" and must be taken to them by the servants of the Lord Jesus Christ, who said, "As the Father has sent me, even so I am sending you" (Matthew 28:19; John 20:21). In one of her hymns Frances Ridley Havergal prays,

> *Take my feet, and let them be*
> *swift and beautiful for thee …*
>
> *Take my lips, and let them be*
> *filled with messages from thee.*

The African-American spiritual urges us to

> *Go, tell it on the mountain,*
> *over the hills and everywhere;*
> *Go, tell it on the mountain*
> *that Jesus Christ is born.*

Christ could not provide salvation for us without great cost; and we cannot take it to the world without paying a price. In a sermon entitled "The Sacrifice of Christ, the Type and Model of Missionary Effort," James Henley Thornwell said, "As Jesus by His sacrifice purchased redemption, we by ours must make it known" (*Collected Works* 2:411-449).

J. Oswald Sanders, Bible teacher and missionary leader from New Zealand, told about an Indian Christian who walked barefoot from village to village preaching the gospel. After a long day and many miles, he came to a village where he tried to preach but was rudely spurned. He went out of the village, lay down under a tree, and fell asleep from sheer exhaustion. He suddenly awoke and saw people looking at him. He thought that they had come to hurt or even kill him. The head man of the village explained that when they saw his blistered and bleeding feet they knew that he must be a holy man. They had been wrong to reject him. They wanted to hear the message that he had walked so far to bring them.

> *How beauteous are their feet*
> *Who stand on Zion's hill!*
> *Who bring salvation on their tongues,*
> *And words of peace reveal!*
> (Isaac Watts)

JOHN ELIOT
(1604–1690)

It is good that such a man has lived.

JOHN ELIOT preached two sermons to the Algonquian Indians in 1646. The first, in September, was a failure. The Indians 'gave no heed to it, but rather were weary, and rather despised what I said,' Eliot wrote.[1] He tried again, in October. A small group of Indians sat in the wigwam of Waban, one of their chiefs, and listened to this white man. Eliot presented the ten commandments and taught the first three questions of the catechism. Then he preached about Ezekiel's vision of the dry bones—a story that apparently pleased the Indians. From there he moved on to all the principal matters of Protestant theology. When he finished and asked for questions, the Indians responded eagerly, asking questions for three hours. The first question was, 'How may we come to know Jesus Christ?' Later an Indian asked John Eliot, 'Why has no white man ever told us this before? Why did you wait to tell us?' Eliot could only answer, 'I am sorry.'

It was sixteen years after the founding of the Massachusetts Bay Colony and fifteen years after John Eliot's arrival in Boston.

John Eliot was born in 1604 in Widford, a small English village on the river Lea, twenty-five miles from London.[2] That part of England had welcomed John Wycliffe's Lollards in the fifteenth century, French Huguenots in the sixteenth century, and by the time of Eliot's birth it had become a centre for Puritanism. John Eliot's parents brought him up 'with the fear of God, the word and prayer.' He entered Jesus College, Cambridge, in 1618, several months before his fourteenth birthday. Many years later, he sent a copy of his Indian Bible to the college, inscribed in Latin words that read in English, 'Accept, Mother, I pray, what a most humble alumnus offers, a son ever having thy prayers.'

John Eliot's mother died in 1620, and a year later his father died. After completing his studies in 1622, John briefly assisted the Puritan preacher Thomas Hooker in his academy at Little Baddow. Eliot lived with Hooker and his family. He wrote: 'To this place was I called through the infinite riches of God's mercy in Christ Jesus to my poor soul, for here the Lord said to my dead soul, live! live! and through the grace of God I do live and shall live forever! When I came to this blessed family I then saw as never before the power of godliness in its lovely vigour and efficacy.'[3]

With Archbishop Laud in power, it was a difficult time for Puritans. In 1630 Thomas Hooker fled to Holland, and the next year John Eliot sailed for the New World.[4] He emigrated, he explained, in order to 'enjoy the holy worship of God, not according to the fantasies of man, but according to the Word of God.'[5] In 1632 John married Hannah Mumford, who had followed him to Massachusetts. We know very little about Hannah, but tradition, writes Ola Winslow, describes her as 'notably resourceful,' given to hospitality, skilful in nursing, and a good manager of house and garden, all valuable assets for a colonial woman, especially one whose husband was often away. 'In her many-faceted partnership in the Eliot home,' writes Winslow, 'she probably deserved the superlatives she inspired.'[6] Hannah and John had six children, one girl and five boys, all of whom followed their parent's example in Christian service.

After serving for six months as a pastor in Boston, mutually pleasant for both preacher and congregation, John Eliot was called to Roxbury, a town nearby that was being settled by some of Eliot's family and friends from England. Winslow thinks that Eliot was ordained in England, although no record of it has been found. The members of the Roxbury church ordained him, making him possibly the first Massachusetts minister who had not been previously ordained by an Anglican bishop.

John Eliot's long ministry of fifty-eight years at the Roxbury church was marked by simple, biblical sermons (so that, Cotton Mather said, 'the lambs of the flock' could understand). 'His standards of Christian character were inflexible,' Winslow writes, 'but his approach to erring ones was unfailingly kind.' His small salary was 'little enough for his needs and never enough for his charities.' Once, so the story goes, the Roxbury deacon presented Eliot with his monthly salary secured in a handkerchief tied with a number of hard knots. On his way home, the pastor called upon a needy widow of his flock. Failing to extract a coin from the stubborn lump, he handed it to her, knots and all, saying, 'Sister, I think the Lord meant it all for you.'[7]

John Eliot was involved in the Anne Hutchinson trials. Nothing harsh is recorded about his part in this difficult and divisive event. His gentleness of manner and kindness of feeling were evident, but he was inflexible in his defence of orthodox doctrine.[8] It was undoubtedly with relief that Eliot turned to a more pleasant task. With other 'good Hebricians,' he was asked to translate some of the Psalms to be included in *The Bay Psalm Book*, the first book printed in English in America.

'In North America, Protestant Christians for the first time lived side by side with a non-Christian people,' writes Andrew Walls. The seal of the Massachusetts Bay Colony depicted an Indian and the words from Acts 16:9, 'Come over and help us.'[9] The colony's charter stated that 'the principal end of this plantation' is 'to win and incite the natives to the knowledge and obedience of the only true God and Saviour of mankind.' 'The initial desire,' Walls writes, 'to bring these people into the Christian fold, while never abandoned, receded before temporal considerations.'[10] The colonists faced the pressing concerns of surviving the rigours of a difficult climate and creating for themselves a pioneer life in New England. The Indians were their neighbours, but neighbours with whom relations were, to say the least, ambivalent. Those colonists who wanted to reach out to the Indians were deterred by the difficulty of learning the Indians' languages. Cotton Mather considered the Algonquian dialect so difficult that demons, he said, who understood Hebrew, Greek, and Latin were unable to fathom it! Prevalent eschatological views (that the millennium would be ushered in by the conversion of the Jews) hindered some from undertaking an aggressive evangelization of the Indians. Furthermore, Congregational church polity did not provide for ordaining persons for full-time missionary service.

The missionary call does not seem to have been a factor in Eliot's emigration to America, but it gradually became important in the Puritan preacher's mind and heart. When asked years later what had moved him to begin work with the Indians, he replied that the 'public engagement' was the colony's seal, and, privately, his own 'pity for the poor Indian.' He never saw the Indians as the 'dregs of humanity' as many others did, but as human beings, created in God's image but lost without Christ. In 1646 the colony and some of the leaders of neighbouring Indian tribes signed an agreement to try to reduce the tensions between the Indians and the English and to bring the two communities closer together. Eliot decided it was time for him to reach out to the Indians.

After his momentous meeting with the Indians in Waban's wigwam in October 1646, John Eliot and three English friends who had come with him decided to continue their visits to the Indians, the winter frosts and snows notwithstanding, lest the 'fire go out of the Indians' hearts for want of a little fuel.'[11]

For the next forty years, in all kinds of weather, the Puritan preacher journeyed by horseback between Sundays to the scattered Indian villages, preaching justification, faith, repentance, and holy living. Eliot preserved the Indians' questions, treating them in his sermons. He became skilled in finding ways to communicate Christian truths in simple ways and with illustrations the Indians could understand. An Indian asked, 'Does the white man's god hear Indian prayers?' Eliot replied, 'Certainly. Look at this basket. You made it. White straws, black straws. You know where they came from, and how you put them together. Someone who didn't make it wouldn't know. He wouldn't understand how you could do it. God made Indians. He knows all about them. Of course, he knows your language and understands every word.'[12]

The Indians asked John Eliot many questions such as: Why didn't God kill the devil that made all men bad, God having all power? Why didn't God give all men good hearts? Where do little children go when they die, seeing they have not sinned? How shall I bring my heart to love prayer? How long was Adam good before he sinned? Does the devil dwell in us as we dwell in a wigwam? When a soul goes to heaven (or hell) what does it say when it gets there? Why does God punish in hell forever? Why must we love our enemies, and how shall we do it? May a good man sin sometimes?

Eliot was encouraged by the Indians' response to his ministry, but wrote in 1648, 'The day of grace is not yet come unto them.' Soon, however, he said, 'In prayer they exceed my expectations.'[13] In fact, those who became Christians were known as 'Praying Indians.' In *John Eliot and the Praying Indians of Massachusetts Bay*, historian Kathryn Gray describes how the Indian women were very important to the success of the mission. 'On many occasions,' she writes, 'it is the nameless mothers and wives who have responded to Eliot's teachings and it is they who make possible the conversion of whole families to Christianity.'[14]

The Indians asked Eliot for land on which to build a town, so the preacher and the Indians began to search for a suitable place. One day Eliot dismounted, tied his horse to a tree, and prayed that God would lead them. While he was on his knees, one of the Indians came down the trail and said to him, 'Come.' He led Eliot to the perfect place. Eliot negotiated with the colony's leaders for six thousand acres, and by 1650 Natick, the first 'Praying Town,' was laid out. John Endicott, governor of the Massachusetts Bay Colony, visited Natick one preaching day late in 1651. He rode forty miles to get there and declared that it was 'one of the best journeys' he had ever made. 'Such reverence, zeal, good affection, and distinct utterance, I could not but admire,' he wrote; 'the foundation is laid, and such a one that I verily believe the gates of hell shall never prevail against.'[15]

There would be thirteen more Praying Towns, most if not all located in sites chosen by the Indians. Instruction in the towns was almost entirely in the hands of the Indians. 'Their own nation trained up and schooled unto ability for the work,' Eliot wrote, 'are the most likely instruments to carry on this work.'[16] By the early 1670s over a thousand Indians were Christians, in testimony to the fruitful ministry of John Eliot. In preparing for self-government of the Praying Towns, Eliot proposed the plan given to Moses by his father-in-law, Jethro, after Moses had led the children of Israel out of the wilderness. It provided for one man for every ten people to judge small matters, another man for every fifty to judge more serious matters, and still another for every hundred people to judge the greatest matters. This plan seemed to work well with the Indians.

A synod of Massachusetts ministers, meeting in May 1647, commissioned one of their number, Edward Winslow, a deeply religious and eminently practical man, to go to England to seek financial help for Eliot's mission to the Indians. Winslow used to good effect lively 'tracts' in which Eliot and some others described the progress and success of the mission. The titles of the first three are *The Day Breaking, if not the Sun Rising of the Gospel with the Indians in New England; The Clear Sunshine of the Gospel Breaking Forth upon the Indians in New England*; and *The Glorious Progress of the Gospel amongst the Indians in New England*. In 1649 English Parliament formed the Society for the Propagation of the Gospel in New England (later known as the New England Company) to support Eliot's work, and during that year twelve thousand pounds were collected in England and Wales, mostly from small donations.[17] Eliot used his writing not only to create interest in the Indian mission, but also to minister to English Christians. In his *Indian Dialogues* he challenges his readers to be instructed and inspired by the same heavenly riches and true wealth that marked the spiritual testimonies of his Indian converts.

John Eliot carried on extensive correspondence with some of the Christian leaders of his time, including Richard Baxter. In his first letter to Baxter, Eliot wrote, 'Now respected and dear Sir, the sense and savour which the Lord hath impressed on my spirit by these your holy labours, doth embolden me to make a motion to you, and a request, that you would spend the rest of your life writing practical meditations.' Although they never met, their friendship began with Eliot's letter in 1656 and lasted until 1691 when the news of Eliot's death reached Baxter.

On September 24, 1651, the Natick Indians adopted a civil covenant with God, written for them by John Eliot:

> We are the sons of Adam. We and our forefathers have a long time been lost in our sins, but now the mercy of God begins to find us out again. Therefore, the grace of Christ helping us, we do give ourselves and our children unto God to be his people; he shall rule us in all affairs, not only in our religion and affairs of the church (these we desire as soon as we can, if God will) but also in all our works and affairs in this world; God shall rule over us. The Lord is our judge, the Lord is our lawgiver, the Lord is our king. He will save us; the wisdom which God has taught us in his books, that shall guide and direct us in the way. Oh Jehovah, teach us wisdom to find out thy wisdom in thy Scriptures, let the grace of Christ help us, because Christ is the wisdom of God, send thy Spirit into our hearts, and let it teach us; Lord take us to be thy people, and let us take thee to be our Lord.[18]

The Natick Indians held worship services from 1651, but they did not have a regular church until 1660, fourteen years after the first preaching service at Waban's wigwam. To 'gather' a church in the Puritan fashion, church leaders heard the testimonies or conversion narratives of the Indians who seemed most promising for church membership. One Indian began: 'I confess in the presence of the

Lord, before I prayed, many were my sins, not one good word did I speak, not one good thought did I think, not one good action did I do.' He continued for some time, ending with the words: 'I confess I deserve hell, I cannot deliver myself, but I give my soul and my flesh to Christ, and I trust my soul with him for he is my Redeemer, and I desire to call upon him while I live.' After giving their testimonies, the Indians were asked questions about the Bible and doctrine. Charles Cohen, an authority on Puritan spirituality, judges that the Indians were 'at least as conversant with essential doctrines as were the goodmen and goodwives of Puritan Massachusetts.'[19]

Despite a busy schedule of ministry in Roxbury and among the Indians, and with no time for extended study except for a few months of illness in 1656, John Eliot translated the whole Bible into the Algonquian language in fourteen years. He replied to those who criticized his undertaking such a time-consuming task, 'The Bible is the word of life. The Indians must have it.'[20]

The Algonquian Bible, published in 1663, was the first Bible printed in any language in the New World. John Eliot possessed natural ability in language study, as well as a good knowledge of Hebrew, Greek, and Latin. Experts have judged that his translation is as good as any first version of the Bible from a previously unwritten language. Eliot's Indian grammar, finished in 1666, is recognized as an important step in the development of linguistic science. Kenneth Miner calls Eliot 'the true founder of American linguistics.'[21]

Eliot wrote *The Indian Grammar Begun* to help missionaries learn the Algonquian language. On the last page of his book, Eliot wrote: 'We must not sit still, and look for miracles; up and be doing, and the Lord be with thee. Prayers and pains, through faith in Christ Jesus, will do anything.'[22] Differing from many of his fellow colonists, Eliot 'truly believed that tribal languages could be languages of Christianity.'[23] His Algonquian grammar was reprinted in 2001, with words of appreciation from present-day Natick descendants. They wrote that Eliot's 'gifts to our people have spanned over 350 years and continue to reach his beloved Praying Indians.'[24]

After the publication of the Indian Bible, Eliot translated into Algonquian books by Richard Baxter (*A Call to the Unconverted*), Thomas Shepard (*The Sincere Convert* and *The Sound Believer*), and Lewis Bayly (*The Practice of Piety*). Eliot wrote to Baxter, 'I believe that it will not be unacceptable to you, that the call of Christ by your holy labours shall be made to speak in the Indians' ears in their own language, that you may preach unto our poor Indians.'[25]

John Eliot became more and more sympathetic to the Indians' problems, helped them in their disputes with other Indians, and promoted their causes with the colony officials. Richard Cogley concludes that John Eliot 'regarded the mission as a way of protecting Native Americans, whether Christian or not, from land-grabbing settlers and from Indian marauders.'[26] Perhaps the Indians could have been guided toward 'civility' without surrendering their traditional culture so completely. Perhaps the Praying Towns could have promoted Christian living on the part of the Indians without segregating them from their pagan relatives. Eliot's work was not perfect, but it was strong and good—and, in an important sense, lasting. It stands as a testimony that 'prayers and pains through faith in Jesus Christ' can do anything.

By the 1670s the missionary work among the Indians was moving steadily forward. Several thousand Indians had confessed their faith in Christ, and native pastors were being trained. Eliot wrote in 1671 that 'all the Massachusetts [Indians] pray' to God.[27] After his sermon one day in 1674, one of the Indian leaders stood up and said that he would become a Christian. He addressed Eliot:

> Sir, you have been pleased for four years past, in your abundant love, to apply yourself particularly unto me and my people, to exhort, press and persuade us to pray to God. I am very thankful to you for your pains. I must acknowledge, I have, all my days, used to pass in an old canoe, and now you exhort me to change and leave my old canoe, and embark in a new canoe, to which I have hitherto been unwilling; but now I yield myself to your advice, and enter into a new canoe, and do engage to pray to God hereafter.[28]

During the years from 1650 to 1675, while John Eliot's fourteen Praying Towns were being settled, other English missionaries were at work in New England. The Mayhew family's ministry on Martha's Vineyard, Nantucket, and adjacent islands was the most successful, reaching many more Indians than John Eliot did on the mainland. Eliot was not in the least jealous. He wrote: 'If any of the human race ever enjoyed the luxury of doing good, if any Christian ever could declare what it is to have peace, not as the world gives, but which surpasses the conception of those who look not beyond the world, we may believe this was the happiness of the Mayhews.'[29]

Throughout John Eliot's long life many visitors came to Roxbury to see him. Eliot welcomed them all. 'He that writes of Eliot,' said Cotton Mather, 'must write of charity or say nothing.'[30] In December 1650 Gabriel Druillette, a Roman Catholic missionary to the Indians on the Kennebek, came to Boston in the hope of persuading the English to join in an alliance against the Mohawks who were harassing his mission. Eliot hosted him for the night. The Puritan and the Jesuit spent the evening discussing missionary strategy and native languages. Neither could speak the other's language, but they conversed in the college Latin of their student days. 'He treated me with respect and kindness,' Druillette recalled, 'and begged me to spend the winter with him.'[31]

Prospects were good for establishing many more Praying Towns, but instead a tragic war between the Indians and the English destroyed almost all of Eliot's work of more than thirty years. Unlike his father, who had befriended the Pilgrims, the Indian King Philip deeply resented the power of the English and the expansion of their settlements into Indian territory. The central issue in the long-slumbering hostility concerned control of land over which the Indians had roamed at will until the colonists arrived. At first the war went against the English, who were not accustomed to Indian ways of fighting. The Indians destroyed English towns and killed many of the towns' inhabitants. It seemed possible, maybe even probable, that the English would be totally defeated.

Distrust of the Indians became anger and rage. All Indians were condemned, even those of the Praying Towns. The Christian Indians were rounded up and exiled to Deer

Island.[32] John Eliot met his people as they left for the island, prayed with them, spoke what comfort he could, and bade them farewell. In his words, 'Harried away to an island at half an hour's warning, poor souls in terror left their goods, books, and Bibles; only some few carried their Bibles, the rest were spoiled and lost.'[33] Winter had come and until wigwams were built there was no shelter on the island and food was scarce. Eliot did what he could, visiting Deer Island several times during the winter. He pled with the English authorities to send food, medicines, and blankets. He experienced abuse and even personal danger because of his efforts to get help for the Praying Indians.

John Eliot protested strongly against the proposal to sell captive Indians into slavery in the West Indies. 'To sell souls for money seems to me a dangerous merchandise,' he wrote to the authorities in Boston. 'I desire the honoured Council to pardon my boldness [and] weigh the reason and religion that laboureth in this great case of conscience.'[34]

The Indian King Philip was killed on August 12, 1676, marking the beginning of the end of active conflict, but settled peace was long in coming. John Eliot's work lay in ruins. He wrote:

> Prayer to God was quenched, the younger generation being debauched by it, and the good old generation of the first beginners gathered home by death. So Satan improved the opportunity to defile, debase, and bring into contempt the whole work of praying to God. A great apostasy defiled us. And yet through grace some stood and do stand, and the work is on foot to this day, praised be the Lord.[35]

In a letter sent to a friend in England, Eliot quoted an Indian woman who described the suffering of the Praying Indians and asked God to help them. Eliot used this woman's testimony to explain that the mission, although damaged and faltering, was not buried, but with help might 'rise again.'[36]

In 1676 Eliot was seventy-two years old. His strength was failing, but he did not give up. He started over and worked another decade, until he was no longer able to make the long horseback journeys to the Indian towns. He wrote to one of the members of the New England Company, 'I can do little, yet I am resolved through the grace of Christ, I will never give over the work, so long as I have legs to go.'[37]

John Eliot was determined to produce another edition of the Algonquian Bible, because almost all copies had been lost or destroyed during the upheavals of war and exile. Both in London and in the Massachusetts Bay there was little support for the undertaking of such an expensive project. Most argued that it was time for the Indians to learn to read the English Bible, but Eliot was insistent. He wrote to influential English friends, such as Richard Baxter, who had a keen interest in the Indian work and a deep respect for John Eliot, asking them to intercede for him with the New England Company. Baxter himself questioned the wisdom of a new edition, but wrote, 'If the old man die first, it is a great doubt whether any will ever perform it. Besides it may be useful.' Eliot did not give up—giving up was unknown to him—and finally the second edition of the entire Algonquian Bible was printed in 1685, 'ending nine years of urgent entreaty, anxiety and of much added labour for John Eliot.' The old man was overjoyed. 'Our Indian work yet liveth,' he wrote. 'The Bible is come forth, many hundreds bound up, and dispersed to the Indians.' Bayly's *The Practice of Piety* was also finished. 'Let us do the primer and the catechism again. I am old, ready to be gone, and desire to leave as many books as I can.'[38]

John Eliot's growing infirmity saddened his Indian friends. They wrote to him in March 1684:

> You are now grown aged, so that we are deprived of seeing your face and hearing your voice (especially in the winter season) so frequently as formerly. God hath made you to us and our nation a spiritual father, and we are inexpressibly [indebted] to you for your faithful constant indefatigable labours, care and love, to and for us, and you have always manifested the same to us as well in our adversity as prosperity, for about forty years making known to us the Glad Tidings of Salvation of Jesus Christ.[39]

Hannah, John Eliot's wife and colleague in ministry, died in 1687. She was, writes Ola Winslow, 'a woman loved and honoured by the whole community she had served these many years. There was hardly a household in the town that did not have cause to thank her for the kindly offices gently rendered during her fifty-five years as the pastor's wife.'[40] Four of John Eliot's five sons (three of whom were also missionaries to the Indians) died before he did.[41] He outlived nearly every prominent first-generation Massachusetts Puritan. Shortly before his death he remarked that the others, 'who had got safe to heaven would suspect him to have gone the wrong way, because he had stayed so long behind them.'[42] In one of the last glimpses we have of John Eliot we see him gathering Black and Indian children around his chair, teaching them how to read and telling them about Jesus.

On May 20, 1690, the eighty-six-year-old 'apostle to the Indians' died. 'There is only one way to finish the record of his earthly story,' wrote Ola Winslow, 'and that is with the two last words he spoke, "Welcome joy."'

'For more than forty years, [John Eliot] spent unnumbered days travelling the forest trails, fording unbridged rivers, his nightly shelter often only a blanket, his food carried in his pocket, as he journeyed once a fortnight to the scattered Indian villages, thirty, forty, even sixty and seventy miles from his Roxbury home.'[43] Nathaniel Hawthorne said of this New England hero, 'It is good for the world that such a man has lived.'[44]

How beautiful are the feet of those
who preach the good news!

DAVID BRAINERD
(1718–1747)

A life of one plan.

THE most frequently reprinted and widely read book by Jonathan Edwards is not *Religious Affections*, *Freedom of the Will*, or *The Nature of True Virtue*, all masterpieces of Christian literature. It is his *Life of David Brainerd*, which became the best-selling religious book in nineteenth-century America and remains in print in a number of editions to the present day.[1] In the preface to a reprint of the *Life of David Brainerd*, Horatius Bonar wrote, 'His life was not a great life, as men use the word,' but it was 'a life of one plan, expending itself in the fulfillment of one great aim, and in the doing of one great deed—serving God.'

David Brainerd was born on April 20, 1718, at Haddam, Connecticut, a son of a 'respected, prosperous family that was very much part of the Connecticut establishment.'[2] When he was nine years old his father died, and five years later, his mother. David went to live with relatives and seemed likely to become a farmer, working land that his father had left to him and his brothers.

As a young man, Brainerd had, as he said, 'a very good outside.' He proceeded 'a considerable length on a self-righteous foundation; and should have been entirely lost and undone, had not the mere mercy of God prevented.'[3] Solomon Stoddard's *Guide to Christ* was 'the happy means' of his conversion. It was not, however, an easy one. Brainerd blamed Stoddard because he did not tell him clearly enough what he could do to come to Christ. He blamed God for his 'cruelty and injustice' in punishing sinners. He blamed himself for his presumption in thinking that he was 'aiming at God's glory' when he was seeking his own happiness. But Stoddard's book worked its way into his heart, and after a period of 'distressed, bewildered, and tumultuous state of mind,' the twenty-year-old Brainerd was radically transformed by a vision of God's glory: 'My soul was so captivated and delighted with the excellency, loveliness, greatness, and other perfections of God, that I was even swallowed up in Him.'[4]

In 1739 Brainerd entered Yale College to prepare for the ministry. He 'enjoyed considerable sweetness in religion,' but soon was disturbed by ambition in his studies, and troubled by bouts of severe illness, including the onset of tuberculosis that would claim his life seven years later. His 'soul was refreshed,' however, by reports of George Whitefield's preaching in New England. He was greatly influenced by Whitefield's sermons in New Haven and those of Gilbert Tennent a few months later. At this time, writes Jonathan Edwards, David Brainerd experienced 'much of God's gracious presence, and of the lively actings of true grace.' Some students, including Brainerd, sought to convert their fellow students and attended 'separatist' meetings in town, despite the college rules. When in a private conversation Brainerd criticized one of the tutors, declaring that he had no more grace than a chair, he was expelled from Yale. Jonathan Edwards appealed to the administration that Brainerd had made 'a truly humble and Christian acknowledgement of his fault,' but the college leaders refused to reconsider their decision.[5] Brainerd was deeply hurt and struggled with his feelings for some time until he was able to love and pray for his 'enemies.'

David Brainerd studied privately with a well-known minister and after several months came before the local ministerial association on July 29, 1742. The association examined Brainerd in Greek, Hebrew, Latin, theology, and philosophy, and listened to a sermon he preached, which, according to historian John Grigg, was 'the sermon of a man who understood the role of compassion and love of God in salvation.'[6] The ministers judged Brainerd to be 'a man of high character' with 'a desire to win souls to Christ.' It commended 'him and his labours to the grace and blessing of God' and recommended him 'to any people among whom God in his providence may call him.'[7]

Brainerd preached for a time in a kind of itinerant ministry, until he was convinced that God was calling him to be a missionary 'to the heathen.'[8] In November 1742 he was invited to New York to meet with the American commissioners of the Society in Scotland for Propagating Christian Knowledge. Brainerd continued with the society during the whole of his short missionary career. An Indian woman asked Brainerd 'whether he was not sent to preach to the Indians by some good people a great way off.' He replied, 'Yes, by the good people in Scotland.' She answered 'that her heart loved those good people so that she could scarce help praying for them all night.'[9]

The American commissioners of the Society in Scotland directed Brainerd to spend a short time as supply minister at a church in Easthampton on Long Island. There he was able to act as a peacemaker between the various factions that disagreed over the revival that was sweeping New England. Brainerd greatly approved of the revival, believing it to be a genuine work of God, but had come to see that it could produce extremes and unhelpful criticism of others. He preached and counselled 'moderation and mildness,' as he would the rest of his life. Jonathan Edwards believed that more than anyone he knew, Brainerd was able to distinguish between the true and the false in the revival. While on Long Island David Brainerd was able to get a taste of his life's work as he preached several times to a Montauk Indian congregation.

Brainerd was sent by the Society commissioners to a small settlement of Mahican Indians at Kaunameek in New York, twenty miles from Stockbridge, Massachusetts, where John Sergeant, who had studied under Jonathan Edwards at Northampton, was at work. Brainerd lived in a wigwam and then in a rough little cottage he built, and attempted, without much success, to learn the Indian language. He was lonely for Christian friends and fellowship and still troubled by the 'party-spirit' that he had exhibited at Yale, and about which he repented and sought God's forgiveness. He preached to the Mahicans and also to 'white' settlers who lived in the area, who 'although they are called Christians,' Brainerd wrote, 'seemed to have no concern for Christ's kingdom.'[10] When the little group of Indians at Kaunameek decided to move to Stockbridge, Brainerd's first ministry ended. Although discouraged with his lack of success in converting the Indians, Brainerd believed that 'truths of God's Word' were, at times, 'attended with some power upon [their] hearts and consciences.'[11]

David Brainerd received calls from a church near his hometown in Connecticut and also from the church at Easthampton on Long Island, which was, according to Jonathan Edwards, 'the fairest, pleasantest, town on the whole island, and one of its largest and most wealthy parishes.'[12] The young missionary struggled with his decision but eventually declined the calls. He still felt that he was to work in places where the gospel had not been preached. He was in New Haven on September 14, 1743, the day he would have received his degree. He feared that he would be 'overwhelmed with perplexity and confusion,' but God enabled him 'with calmness and resignation, to say, "The will of the Lord be done."'[13] Jonathan Edwards, who was also in New Haven, met Brainerd for the first time. 'There truly appeared in him,' Jonathan Edwards wrote, 'a great degree of calmness and humility' despite the injustice he had received.[14] In his diary for March 12, 1744, Brainerd wrote, 'I longed that those who, I have reason to think, owe me ill will, might be eternally happy. It seemed refreshing to think of meeting them in heaven, how much soever they had injured me on earth.'[15]

The commissioners of the Scottish Society sent Brainerd to the Indians at the Forks of the Delaware in Pennsylvania. He arrived on May 12, 1744, and, for almost three years, worked among the Indians and settlers who lived in the Delaware Valley, in nearby areas in New Jersey, and at several locations along the Susquehanna River. He struggled with the intricate dialects of several Indian languages, with physical weariness and illness, and with deep distrust on the part of the Indians, who had so often suffered at the hands of white men. But God was 'pleased to support my sinking soul,' Brainerd wrote, so that I 'never entertained any thought of quitting my business among the poor Indians.'[16]

Like his contemporaries in general, David Brainerd had little sympathy for the customs of the Native Americans and referred to them as 'rude savages' and 'poor pagans.' He wished that the Indians would adopt a more settled and 'civilized' way of life, but, as missiologist Andrew Walls wrote, 'he was in no danger of identifying regeneration and civilization.'[17] There are some indications in his diary and journal that he became more accepting of some Indian attitudes and practices. Once when he was on a missionary journey to the Susquehanna, he encountered a 'shaman' in a colored mask with a hideous appearance approaching him, dancing with a calabash in his hand. 'Of all the sights I ever saw,' Brainerd wrote, 'none appeared so frightful, so near akin to what is imagined of "infernal powers."' Later, when he was sitting down with the same 'shaman,' Brainerd found in him a reforming prophet who believed he had been called by his god to summon people to repentance from their evil ways. 'Some of his sentiments seemed very just,' Brainerd wrote, and 'there was something in his temper and disposition which looked more like true religion than anything I have ever discovered among other heathens.'[18] Brainerd had less than three years to live with the Indians. If he had lived longer he may have moved much further in his understanding and appreciation of these people, as John Eliot did in his long ministry with the Algonquians in Massachusetts.

In 1744 the Presbytery of New York of the New Side Presbyterian Church ordained Brainerd, and the next year he moved to New Jersey to preach to the Indians at Crossweeksung, suspended as he was, he said, 'between hope and fear.'[19] Moses Tattamy, Brainerd's faithful Indian translator, and his wife were converted. Brainerd asserted that 'my interpreter was amazingly assisted, and I doubt not but the Spirit of God was upon him.'[20] Tattamy became, observes John Grigg, one of the keys 'in the future course of Brainerd's ministry.' He 'was able to translate Brainerd's words in a way that reflected not only Brainerd's content but his style of preaching.'[21] Brainerd reported to the Scottish Society that Tattamy's 'heart echoes to the soul-humbling doctrines of grace, and he never appears better pleased than when he hears of the absolute sovereignty of God, and the salvation of sinners in a way of mere free grace.'[22]

Brainerd described a change in the emphasis of his preaching to the Indians:

> The more I discoursed of the love and compassion of God in sending his Son to suffer for the sins of men, and the more I invited them to come and partake

of his love, the more their distress was aggravated, because they felt themselves unable to come. It was surprising to me to see how their hearts seemed to be pierced with the tender and melting invitations of the Gospel, when there was not a word of terror [that is, law and judgment] spoken to them.[23]

Typical of his preaching to the Indians at this time was a sermon on Revelation 22:17, 'Whosoever will, let him take the water of life freely.' Brainerd wrote that God enabled him 'in a manner somewhat uncommon to set before them the Lord Jesus Christ as a kind and compassionate Saviour, inviting distressed and perishing sinners to accept everlasting mercy.'[24]

Jonathan Edwards had the same emphasis in his preaching when he went to the Indians at Stockbridge.[25] In a sermon on Revelation 3:20, Edwards pictured a bleeding Christ standing at the door and knocking. 'Let him in,' Edwards pled. 'Will you shut him out when he comes to you and knocks at your door with his wounded, bleeding hands?'[26] Edwards ended with this moving invitation:

Christ has provided a great feast, set the door wide open, and says, 'Whosoever will may come.' You may come and eat without money, come for nothing. Christ has paid the price, and you may come for nothing. You may have Christ for your Saviour and may have all heaven but only come to Christ with all your heart. Christ stands at the door and knocks. If you will open the door, he will come in, and he will give himself to you and all that he has.[27]

There came to the Indians at Crossweeksung what Brainerd called 'an amazing season of grace.'[28] He baptized those whom he was convinced had experienced saving grace. Brainerd wrote: 'Never did I see such an appearance of Christian love among any people in all my life. It was so remarkable that one might well have cried with an agreeable surprise, "Behold, how they love one another!"'[29] Some of the women made journeys of ten and fifteen miles to invite others to hear Brainerd preach. They came, and Brainerd's audience grew to almost a hundred. Iain Murray writes that this was a true awakening, 'one of the most remarkable in Christian history.'[30] Now an ordained Presbyterian minister, Brainerd conducted a Communion season in the Scottish sacramental tradition. Two days of preparation were given to preaching, prayer, and repentance, and a day of thanksgiving followed the Communion service itself. Twenty-three Indians received the Communion, and many more attended the services.

During the last year of his life, Brainerd made several journeys from New Jersey to the Forks of the Delaware in Pennsylvania, and then more than a hundred miles further to the scattered Indian settlements along the Susquehannah River. He took some of his Delaware converts with him, who played a vital role in convincing previously resistant Indians to listen anew to the claims of Christianity. The congregation at Crossweeksung organized prayer meetings for their pastor while he was away. Willian Tennent, minister at nearby Freehold, preached to them in Brainerd's absence.

To extend and establish his ministry, Brainerd asked the Scottish society for a colleague to accompany him to distant preaching posts, and for a school to enable him to build a church of mature Christians. As a step in this direction, Brainerd began lectures based on the Westminster Shorter Catechism. He was pleasantly surprised to find the Indians' "doctrinal knowledge to exceed his own expectations." His fears that the catechetical method would "tend only to enlighten the head, but not affect the heart" were unfounded. He wrote that when I 'discoursed to my people in the catechetical method,' God 'granted a remarkable influence of His blessed Spirit to accompany what was spoken, and a great concern appeared in the assembly.'[31]

In May 1746 the New Jersey Indians who were scattered around Crossweeksung moved to Cranbury, New Jersey, where Brainerd hoped God would settle them 'as a Christian congregation.'[32] The Indians were granted land near Cranbury, but some whites strenuously opposed the settlement and tried to find ways to seize the Indians' land.

A final missionary trip to the Susquehanna in August 1746 was interrupted by illness, and Brainerd returned to Cranbury, doubting that he would recover but 'little exercised with melancholy, as in former seasons of weakness.' He was, he wrote, 'willing either to die or live; but found it hard to be reconciled to the thoughts of living useless. Oh, that I might never live to be a burden to God's creation, but that I might be allowed to repair home when my sojourning work is done!'[33]

In March 1747 Brainerd visited his congregation at Cranbury for the last time, then journeyed to Newark where he spent the winter months in the home of Jonathan Dickinson, who was organizing the College of New Jersey, of which Dickinson became the first president.[34] In the spring, Brainerd traveled on to the home of Jonathan Edwards in Massachusetts.

Jonathan Edwards was drawn to the young man. He wrote, 'I found him remarkably sociable, pleasant, and entertaining in his conversation; yet solid, savoury, spiritual and very profitable. He appeared meek, modest and humble, far from any stiffness, moroseness, superstitious demureness, or affected singularity in speech or behaviour.'[35] Edwards never heard Brainerd preach, but, during his months in Edwards' home, he often heard him pray. Edwards wrote, 'I think his manner of addressing himself to God almost inimitable, such (so far as I may judge) as I have rarely known equaled.'[36]

It was a busy time in the Edwards household, but daughter Jerusha gladly gave herself to the task of caring for the sick missionary. In June, she accompanied Brainerd on a trip to Boston, but his illness prevented his doing much except for a little writing. To his brother John, also a missionary among the Indians of New Jersey, he wrote, 'I declare, now I am dying, I would not have spent my life otherwise for the whole world.'[37] On July 6, 1744, Brainerd wrote in his diary, 'Last year, I longed to be prepared for a world of glory and speedily to depart out of this world; but of late all my concern almost is for the conversion of the heathen, and for that end I long to live. And when I long for holiness now it is not so much for myself as formerly, but rather that thereby I may become an "able minister of the New Testament," especially to the heathen.'[38]

In his final days, Brainerd corrected some of his private writings and gave spiritual counsel to those about him. He spoke to the younger Edwards children, 'one by one,' much to the delight of their father. He told his friends goodbye. When Jerusha came into his room, he said,

> Dear Jerusha, are you willing to part with me? I am quite willing to part with you: I am willing to part with all my friends: I am willing to part with my dear brother John; although I love him best of any creature living: I have committed him and all my friends to God, and can leave them with God. Though, if I thought I should not see you and be happy with you in another world, I could not bear to part with you. But we shall spend a happy eternity together.

There is no evidence that David Brainerd and Jerusha were engaged to be married, as is sometimes claimed, but their story, writes George Marsden, is 'one of history's fabled spiritual love tales.'[39]

A little before he died, Brainerd said to Edwards, 'As I waked out of sleep I was led to cry for the pouring out of God's Spirit and the advancement of Christ's kingdom, for which the dear Redeemer died and suffered so much.'[40] The last entry in Brainerd's diary, dictated to his brother Israel on October 2, reads: 'My soul was this day at turns sweetly set on God: I longed to be "with Him" that I might "behold His glory."'[41]

David Brainerd died on October 9, 1747, at the age of twenty-nine. The funeral was simple, as Brainerd had requested. Edwards preached on 'True Saints, When Absent from the Body, are Present with the Lord.' He said that Brainerd lived 'as one who had indeed sold all for Christ, and had entirely devoted himself to God, and made his glory his highest end.' His soul, said Edwards, 'as we may well conclude, was received by his dear Lord and Master, as an eminently faithful servant, into that state of perfection and fruition of God, which he had so often and so ardently longed for; and was welcomed by the glorious assembly in the upper world, as one peculiarly fitted to join them in their blessed employments and enjoyments.'[42]

Brainerd put his writings in Jonathan Edwards' hands and asked him to dispose of them as 'would be most for God's glory and the interest of religion.' Setting aside other important projects, Edwards edited these writings, added his own comments, and published them in 1749 as *An Account of the Life of David Brainerd*. Despite his omissions and summaries, and his commentary on certain statements and experiences of Brainerd's, 'the essential message he conveyed in the Life of Brainerd was true to its subject,' claims John Grigg.[44]

Brainerd's writings included both a private diary and a public journal. According to Marcus Loane:

> The diary is a remarkable record of the interior life of the soul, and its entries still throb with the tremendous earnestness of a man whose heart was aflame for God. The journal is an objective history of the missionary work of twelve months, and its details are an astonishing testimony to the grace of God. Each needs to be studied as the revelation of a Christian character as rare as it was real.[45]

Edwards began his *Life of David Brainerd* with a classic sentence: 'There are two ways of representing and recommending true religion and virtue to the world; the one, doctrine and precept, the other is by instance and example.' Edwards was careful to make clear that Brainerd was not perfect. He pointed out that Brainerd was 'by his constitution and natural temper, prone to melancholy and dejection of spirit.'[46] In many entries in his diary Brainerd expressed a deep sense of his own unworthiness. At one place he wrote, 'My spiritual conflicts today were unspeakably dreadful, heavier than the mountains and overflowing floods. I seemed enclosed, as it were, in hell itself.'[47] A little later he wrote, 'I was greatly exercised with inward trials and distresses all day. In the evening, my heart was sunk and I seemed to have no God to go to.'[48] Brainerd never fully escaped the desolation of depression, but toward the end of his life he found some relief. He began to realize that his 'dejection' was 'very much related to [his] bodily weakness and disorder.' He wrote, 'God was pleased to remove the gloom which has of late oppressed my mind and give me freedom and sweetness in prayer. I was encouraged, strengthened, and enabled to plead for grace for myself and mercy for my poor Indians.'[49]

Edwards also faulted Brainerd for being 'excessive in his labors' and 'not taking due care to proportion his fatigues to his strength.'[50] Brainerd drove himself mentally, emotionally, and spiritually. He feared wasting time and becoming useless. He wrote, 'I find it impossible to enjoy peace and tranquility of mind without a careful improvement of time.'[51] He later wrote, 'God does not suffer me to please or comfort myself with hopes of seeing friends, returning to my dear acquaintances, and enjoying worldly comforts.'[52] Again he wrote, 'When I was thus exposed to cold and rain, I was ready to please myself with the thoughts of enjoying a comfortable house, a warm fire, and other outward comforts. But now these have less place in my heart (through the grace of God), and my eye is more to God for comfort.'[53] Brainerd slowly became convinced that God permitted times of relaxation and fellowship with friends. He wrote on April 30, 1745,

> Oh, how heavily does time pass away when I can do nothing to any good purpose but seem obliged to trifle away precious time! But of late, I have seen it my duty to divert myself by all lawful means, that I may be fit, at least some small part of my time, to labor for God. And here is the difference between my present diversions and those I once pursued, when in a natural state. Then I made a god of diversions, delighted in them with a neglect of God, and drew my highest satisfaction from them. Now I use them as a means to help me in living to God, fixedly delighting in Him. Then they were my all; now they are only means leading to my all.[54]

Jonathan Edwards believed that David Brainerd's life showed the right way to success in the work of the ministry: by his example of working diligently, praying, denying himself, and enduring hardness with resolution and patience. In his life work and in his prayer life, Brainerd fulfilled Christ's call to be a missionary. His prayers focused on the conversion of the lost and the establishment of Christ's kingdom throughout the world. It is doubtful whether anybody ever prayed more consistently and earnestly the second petition of the Lord's Prayer, 'Thy kingdom come.' In one of his last prayers, Brainerd said,

'Oh, that God may be glorified in the whole earth! "Lord, let thy kingdom come."'[55]

Edwards' *Life of David Brainerd* revealed a missionary hero whose impact was astounding. The book made a significant contribution to the new era of missions that sent British and American Christians to many parts of the world. It was 'cherished as an inspiring devotional book, and second only to the Bible, by virtually every Protestant missionary in the nineteenth century.'

Edwards intended, however, that Brainerd's life be read not only as an example of a true missionary but also as an example of a real Christian—'a remarkable instance of true and eminent Christian piety in heart and practice.'[57] The heart of Edwards' *Life of David Brainerd*, states George Marsden, was Brainerd's 'example of world-sacrificing piety for a cause of infinite worth.'[58] Edwards had already dealt with the matter of true religion biblically and theologically in *The Distinguishing Marks of the Work of the Spirit of God* (1741) and *The Treatise Concerning Religious Affections* (1746). In 1749 he published Brainerd's *Life*. The book, writes Marsden, 'is *Religious Affections* in the form of a spiritual biography.'[59]

Throughout Brainerd's writings one finds precious gems of Christian truth, often eloquently expressed.

> My soul will be astonished at the unsearchable riches of divine grace when I arrive at the mansions, which the blessed Saviour is gone before to prepare.

> Oh, the closest walk with God is the sweetest heaven that can be enjoyed on earth!

Tonight, I enjoyed a sweet hour with God; I was lifted above the frowns and flatteries of this lower world.

Felt in myself much sweetness and affection in the things of God. Blessed be God for every such divine gale of His Spirit, to speed me on in my way to the new Jerusalem!

Time appeared but an inch long, and eternity at hand.

Filling up our time with and for God is the way to rise up and lie down in peace.

Nothing seemed too hard for God to perform; nothing too great for me to hope for from Him.

I am now more sensible than ever that God alone is 'the author and finisher of our faith,' that is, that the whole and every part of sanctification and every good word, work, and thought found in me, is the effect of His power and grace.

I went on, confiding in God, and fearing nothing so much as self-confidence.

To an eye of reason, everything that respects the conversion of [the Indians] is as dark as midnight; and yet I cannot but hope in God for the accomplishment of something glorious among them.

There are many with whom I can talk about religion; but alas! I find few with whom I can talk religion itself. But blessed be the Lord, there are some that love to feed on the kernel, rather than the shell.

I felt now pleased to think of the glory of God and longed for heaven as a state where I might glorify God perfectly, rather than a place of happiness for myself.

Marilynne Robinson writes:

> I was very struck by something that I came across in my reading of Jonathan Edwards. I recall him quoting a writer who talks about how whatever we say lives on after us, that we continue to exist so long as any word we say exists in a living mind. And that there should be two judgments: one when we die, and one when the full impact of our lives has played itself out.[61]

The full impact of David Brainerd's life is still playing itself out. John Piper writes:

> I thank God for the ministry of David Brainerd in my own life—the passion for prayer, the spiritual feast of fasting, the sweetness of the Word of God, the unremitting perseverance through hardship, the relentless focus on the glory of God, the utter dependence on grace, the final resting in the righteousness of Christ, the pursuit of perishing sinners, the holiness while suffering, the fixing the mind on what is eternal, and finishing well without cursing the disease that cut him down at twenty-nine.[62]

David Brainerd was a missionary who could never rest until he made one more journey into the dangerous wilderness, seeking the Indians who needed to hear the wonderful good news of the gospel.

How beautiful are the feet of those
who preach the good news!

3

JOHN LEIGHTON WILSON
(1809–1886)

Shall we not go for the love of Christ?

'ONCE on a journey,' John Leighton Wilson wrote, 'under the equatorial suns of Africa, sick, weary, and exhausted, I threw myself down in the shade of a tree, feeling that this might be the place where I would breathe my last, when suddenly a bright light seemed to shine around me, and lit up the tree under which I was lying.' He 'arose, refreshed and invigorated,' and continued on his missionary venture.[1] Wilson, wrote Henry H. Bucher Jr, was 'one of the most eminent American churchmen of the nineteenth century … There is no question that he was a rare combination of apostle, philosopher, linguist, and explorer.'[2] But, above all, he was a missionary—and a missionary statesman.

John Leighton Wilson was a descendant of the Scots-Irish colony of Presbyterians who settled along South Carolina's Black River in 1734.[3] 'Godly folk they were,' writes John Wells, 'worshipping God, reading His Word, keeping

His day, and bringing up their children in the nurture and admonition of the Lord.'[4] William Wilson married Jane James and they became the parents of John Leighton, born on March 25, 1809. Their son 'was a Wilson in humility of soul, simplicity of life, loveliness of character, and consecration to the church; but it was the Jameses' blood coursing through his veins that made him a Joshua to the Southern Church in her days of poverty and desolation.'[5]

John grew up in the low country of South Carolina, a land interlaced with swamps through which flowed sluggish creeks and rivers turned brown by juniper and cypress trees. The higher ground was covered with forests of longleaf pine and giant oaks. In this part of South Carolina were found farms and many slaves. As a child, John's imagination was stirred as he listened in the slaves' cabins to stories about Africa.

Wilson finished his preparatory studies at the well-respected Mount Zion College, a secondary school in Winnsboro, South Carolina. Rejecting South Carolina College because of its 'atheistic' influences, he went to Union College in Schenectady, New York, where fellow South Carolinian John Adger became his best friend. Adger was a major influence in Wilson's decision to enter the ministry and to become a missionary. After graduating from Union, Adger went to Princeton Seminary, and Wilson came home to South Carolina to study at the newly founded Columbia Seminary. Wilson's uncle, Robert Wilson James, pastor of the Salem Black River Presbyterian Church, was one of the founders of the seminary. Robert James preached not only to his white congregation but also to slaves who came in large numbers from nearby plantations to hear his sermons.

In January 1831, Wilson entered Columbia Seminary. His early reading at the seminary included the works of Richard Baxter, John Newton, and Jonathan Edwards's *Life of David Brainerd*. The southwest corner room of the ground floor of the seminary building became 'a place of peculiar sanctity' for Wilson, because it was there that he learned 'what consecration to God meant' as he knelt in prayer with Dr George Howe, his teacher.[6]

John Leighton Wilson grew up with a love for Africa, a continent largely neglected at that time by Christian missionaries. In 1848 Wilson published a short treatise, in which he argued that 'the presence and superintendence of white missionaries are indispensably necessary' in Africa, at least for some years until the African church could carry on the work on its own. Wilson wished there were sufficient 'coloured men from these United States or from the West Indies' to take the gospel to Africa, but that was not yet the case. In the meantime, it was necessary for white men and women to go, despite the dangers. 'Self-denial and personal sacrifices, on the part of friends of the Redeemer, are the chief, and almost the only, means by which his kingdom is advanced in this world,' Wilson wrote.[7]

John Wilson's father at first refused to give his consent for his son to go to Africa as a missionary. 'Father,' said John one day, 'would you be willing to pray the Lord's Prayer with me?' His father agreed and so they began, 'Our Father which art in Heaven, hallowed be thy name. Thy kingdom come. Thy will be done, on earth as it is in heaven.' Brought face to face with the world-embracing love and purpose of God, William Wilson could no longer resist. Slipping his arm around his son's shoulders, he told him he could go.[8]

On September 8, 1833, Harmony Presbytery met at Mount Zion Presbyterian Church to ordain John Leighton Wilson as a foreign missionary. John's uncle, Robert Wilson James, preached the ordination sermon and Dr Howe gave the charge. That afternoon the newly ordained minister preached to the slaves. Afterwards an old man came up to John and said that he believed it was in answer to his prayers that Wilson was going as a missionary to Africa, and that he would 'add to his prayers one dollar for the spread of the gospel' in Africa.[9] Not everyone, however, understood or sympathized with Wilson's plan. He went away as a missionary to Africa, according to Dr Howe, 'amid misconceptions, sneers, and bitter words on the part of many.'[10]

While he was a student at Columbia Seminary, John heard about two sisters in Savannah, Georgia, Jane and Margaret Bayard. They were born on their mother's plantation on Cumberland Island, a lovely isolated place off the coast of Georgia. Both their parents died when they were little girls. The Bayard sisters were popular, talented, wealthy young women, and dedicated members of Savannah's Independent Presbyterian Church. They both wanted to go to the Sandwich Islands as missionaries, but the American Board of Commissioners for Foreign Missions would not accept them because it did not send unmarried women to foreign mission fields. John decided that it was worth going to Savannah to meet the Bayard sisters. Since he was set on a missionary career himself, he was interested in these young women who had 'made up their mind to the work of missions with no parents to say they shall not go.'[11]

John's first sight of Jane came when she was teaching a

class at the African Sunday School sponsored by the Independent Church. She was tall, slender, and graceful, with light hair, blue eyes, and a winsome smile. Two weeks later he was writing to her that she was 'now the nearest and dearest object to my heart on the face of the earth.' 'I cannot be induced to turn away my eyes from Africa,' he wrote. 'My heart is fixed upon that injured, neglected people, and I rejoice that yours is also. We must be subject to many trials and deprivations, but, Jane, this is food for the children of God. Englishmen can penetrate the heart of the country for wealth, and shall we not go for the love of Christ?'[12]

In 1833 Wilson studied Arabic at Andover Seminary and made an exploratory trip to western Africa. Aboard ship he taught Bible to children and adults, and studied Greek, Hebrew, and medicine. He had been offered the position of governor of Liberia. He wrote to Jane that he loved 'the privilege of preaching the gospel too much to give [the offer] a serious consideration.'[13]

On May 21, 1834, John Leighton Wilson and Jane Bayard were married. A few weeks later they departed for Cape Palmas, Liberia, as missionaries with the American Board of Commissioners for Foreign Missions. After arriving in Africa, Wilson wrote to a friend:

> We anchored at Goree after a voyage of thirty days. The sight of land, and especially of the continent of Africa, was refreshing to us, yet not without melancholy reflections. Goree, like many other spots on the coast of Africa, has been the scene of much inhumanity and cruelty. It was once a most extensive slave-market, and although the trade has been suppressed at this place for many years, I fancied I

could almost see traces of human guilt upon her mouldered wall. Indeed, the stone walls which were originally reared to confine the slaves still remain, a monument to the sufferings of the Africans and the reproach of the Christian name.[14]

The Wilsons' mission station—they named it 'Fair Hope'—was beautifully situated near the ocean. To the north stretched a plain of grass through which wound a stream. Wilson wrote, 'I do not know that I have ever seen any place where beauty and grandeur of nature are more harmoniously united.'[15] The Wilsons planted a church, started a school, developed a system of writing for the Glebo language, and translated parts of the scriptures. Wilson soon changed his mind about the American-sponsored colonization movement that led to the founding of Liberia. He believed that it had not only failed to accomplish the good its supporters expected, but had created 'immeasurable evils' in the country.[16]

In 1842, after nine years at Cape Palmas, the American Board moved the Wilsons to Gabon, within the territory north of the Congo River claimed by France. John and Jane turned over their work in Liberia to the Protestant Episcopal Church and launched a new mission among the Mpongwe people. Wilson, a gifted linguist, learned the Mpongwe language, prepared a grammar and dictionary, and wrote and published the first books in that language.[17] Wilson explored western Africa, eventually publishing his findings in the book *Western Africa: Its History, Condition, and Prospects.* David Livingstone pronounced it the best book that had been written about western Africa.[18] A member of the

Royal Oriental Society of Great Britain, Wilson became an established authority on the fauna and flora of Africa.

Wilson developed a respect for 'the variety, integrity, and basic coherence of African cultures.'[19] He praised the traditional Glebo government, finding it so different from 'the arbitrary despotism which prevails in certain parts of Africa, that it may be regarded as the purist specimen of republicanism to be found in the world.'[20] Henry Bucher explored Wilson's role in the initial resistance by the African peoples, among whom Wilson lived, to the beginnings of European colonialism. In Liberia Wilson 'supported the grievances of the Glebo against [black] American colonists in a situation that was legally complicated and emotionally charged with several complex racial issues.'[21] The Glebo, Wilson wrote, 'have been wronged, they have been oppressed and trampled in the dust, and to such a degree as to have wrought in their minds the utmost disgust and hatred for the [American] colony.'[22] In Gabon the Wilsons supported the Mpongwe people against French colonial ambitions.

John Leighton Wilson valued the presence of European nations in Africa for their support of mission work. Because of the protection of the British anti-slavery squadron off the coast of western Africa, Wilson wrote, 'the gospel is statedly preached to thousands, not only along the frontier regions, but far in the interior.'[23] He rejected the idea, however, that civilization and commerce must precede Christianity in evangelizing Africa. 'Commerce, indispensable as it is if unattended by Christianity,' he wrote, 'will be more likely to injure than to benefit people.'[24] Christian missionaries, Wilson said, often 'find themselves in circumstances where duty to the heathen compels them to protest against the measures and designs' of foreign nations.[25]

The longer Wilson was in Africa, the more critical he became of the European role on the continent. It had destroyed, he believed, some of the positive elements of African culture, and had made some deplorable practices, such as slavery, worse. He felt keenly the tragedy of slavery. On a journey to the interior in 1836, he wrote,

> How affecting to trace the footsteps of white men in Africa! I have reference to slave-dealers, who form the great majority of those who have visited her shores! They are to be traced in wars, in bloodshed, in tumults, in distress, in misery, and in everything that can degrade and render savage the heart of man.[26]

'God reigns, and this vile traffic in human beings must come to an end,' Wilson believed.[27] 'Ending the slave trade,' he wrote hopefully in 1852, 'will be regarded as one of the most noble achievements of the nineteenth century.'[28] When there was a move in England to withdraw the British fleet from its patrol of the waters off the African shore because it was felt by many to be accomplishing nothing, Wilson objected. He wrote a long paper that was printed in England in an edition of 10,000 copies and widely distributed in prominent circles. Wilson's voice, claimed his biographer, Hampden DuBose, 'was heard by the English nation.' Many of her people agreed with Wilson's three conclusions: first, that the blockade had done much good for Africa; second, that it must be continued until its work was accomplished; and third, that the fastest ships must be placed in this service.[29] By his writings and persistence, the

South Carolinian played an important role in the permanent suppression of the African slave trade.

Wilson deplored slavery in America, pointing out that 100,000 slaves in the United States meant the death of 150,000 other human beings in the total slave enterprise. He wrote that 'it is an undeniable fact, that much of the misery and wretchedness of that people has been inflicted upon them by ourselves, or by our forefathers.'[30]

Jane Bayard Wilson and her sister freed the thirty slaves they had inherited, giving them the choice 'to go to the North, to Africa, or to any other place where they could enjoy their freedom.'[31] John and Jessie, two slaves whom John had inherited when he turned twenty-one, refused to be emancipated, causing a difficult problem for the Wilsons. When the mission board put pressure on Wilson after Northern newspapers claimed that he was a common slaveholder, he asked if he should force his slaves to be free, noting subtly the irony of such a suggestion. He drew up an emancipatory document for the two slaves and mailed it to his father. Wilson wrote to Rufus Anderson, secretary of the American Board of Commissioners for Foreign Missions, that he had 'used every means, short of coercion, to induce them to go where they could safely accept their freedom.'[32] John and Jessie, however, chose to remain on the Wilson farm as hired labour.[33] Wilson's handling of this situation caused some extremists in the South to regard him as 'a rampant abolitionist' and some in the North continued to denounce him as 'a vile slave-holder, or, to use their modest language, man stealer,' Wilson wrote.[34]

In 1848 Wilson contributed an article to the *Southern Presbyterian Review* on 'The Moral Condition of Western

Africa.' Nothing, Wilson stated—not 'the suppression of the slave trade, as devoutly as this object is to be desired,' nor 'the development of commercial resources'—would change the moral condition of Africa except the preaching of the gospel. He believed that if the Africans 'shall be among the last to receive the blessings of the Gospel, they will be unsurpassed in their devout and steady adherence to the cause of their Saviour.' This statement, which seemed hopelessly optimistic in Wilson's time, has proven to be true in our own.

Because of his wife's failing health and his own, the Wilsons returned to the United States in 1852, after serving almost twenty years in Africa. The Presbytery of Harmony chose him as a commissioner to the General Assembly of 1853. The assembly elected him secretary of the Board of Foreign Missions of the Presbyterian Church, offices of which were located in New York City. Wilson strengthened the mission commitment of the Presbyterian Church. He played a major role in the beginning of the mission to Brazil by supporting Ashbel Green Symington's desire to be sent to that country. He convinced the board that because Symington's 'mind and heart were so strongly drawn to [Brazil's] evangelization, that should be regarded as the guiding hand of Providence.'[35] Wilson was often encouraged, but sometimes found it a hard thing, he said, 'to have to stand between a dying world and an indifferent, hesitating church.'[36]

In 1859 when some Southerners were pressing to legalize the slave trade, Wilson wrote an article for the *Southern Presbyterian Journal* on 'The Foreign Slave Trade: can it be revived without violating the most sacred principles of honour, humanity and religion?'[37] Wilson appealed to his fellow Southerners to act as decent human beings and as Christians.

> We have too high an estimate of the good sense, the Christian moderation, and the honourable bearing of the Southern people, to believe that they ever will, either from motives of retaliation, or the hope of gain, lend their countenance knowingly to the revival of a traffic which, in its progress, must necessarily trample in the dust every sentiment of honour, humanity, and religion.

Many Southerners and others had persuaded themselves that slavery was good for Africans, by bringing them civilization and Christianity. As a Presbyterian Wilson believed that God rules and overrules everything that happens, as the Westminster Confession of Faith states, but he was adamant that God's providence cannot be made a guide for our conduct. Resuming the slave trade is not only to practice a deception among ourselves, Wilson asserted, but is virtually doing evil that good may come, and thus sanctioning the Jesuit dogma that the end justifies the means.

John Leighton Wilson fought the slave trade and hated slavery. He freed his own slaves and worked hard to convince the British to continue their blockade of the ports in western Africa from which slaves were transported to the Americas. In his fight against slavery he did not speak as an abolitionist to denounce sinners but as a Christian to persuade and warn his fellow Southerners that slavery was evil and would lead to disastrous consequences. In 1849, when he was a missionary in Gabon, West Africa, he wrote in the *Southern Presbyterian Review*:

> No people, however great and prosperous, can continue so long, who practically disregard those great laws of Christian charity which were intended to bind the whole human family in one common brotherhood: and a career of reckless disregard for the rights and interests of others can scarcely fail to result in the overthrow of our own.[38]

When the clouds of civil war darkened, John and Jane Wilson packed up in New York and, on the last day the trains were running to the South, returned to the old Wilson homestead in South Carolina 'to suffer with our people.'[39] A close friend, Charles Hodge of Princeton Seminary, who was related to Jane Bayard Wilson, sadly remarked: 'Our wisest man is gone out from us.'[40]

Wilson visited Indian Territory (in the present state of Oklahoma) occupied by five principal tribes which had already cast in their lot with the South. He wrote, 'The Indian tribes, in the providence of God, have been thrown upon the care of the Southern Church.' At a time when access to distant nations was closed this seemed to the organizing Southern Presbyterians 'a clear foreshadowing of the divine purpose to make our beloved church an eminently missionary church, and a heart-stirring call upon all her people to engage in this blessed work with new zeal and self-denial.'[41]

The first General Assembly of the Southern Presbyterian Church met in December 1861 at the First Presbyterian Church in Augusta, Georgia. 'The Assembly began its work,' wrote John Wells, 'with quiet dignity by declaring that the work of preaching the gospel in all the world is the chief work of the Southern Presbyterian Church.'[42] Led by Wilson, the General Assembly stated that it desired distinctly and deliberately to inscribe 'on our church's banner, as she now unfurls it to the world, Christ's last command: 'Go ye into all the world and preach the gospel to every creature.'

The 1863 General Assembly gave Wilson the work of home missions, as well as the task of evangelizing the Southern army. Near the close of the war, Wilson was with the Confederate troops near Petersburg, Virginia. One windy day in March, according to Robert Lewis Dabney, Wilson preached to a South Carolina regiment in the trenches and administered the Lord's Supper 'under a dropping picket fire.' The day following, Wilson met with General Robert E. Lee 'concerning the spiritual wants of the army.'[43] Looking back over the war, Wilson wrote in 1865:

> We should ever be grateful to Almighty God for the repeated and abundant out-pouring of his Holy Spirit upon our armies during the progress of the bloody conflict. That our camps should have been made nurseries of piety is something not only new and unprecedented in warfare, but [this] may be regarded as an encouraging token of God's purpose to favour and bless our future Zion.[44]

During the critical days after the end of the Civil War, the people in the burned city of Columbia were hungry. One who came to help was 'Uncle John,' the emancipated slave who had refused to leave the Wilson homestead. He brought a load of provisions fifty miles through the High

Hills of the Santee and across the Congaree River, to feed those who were living in the seminary buildings. Wilson praised John's faithfulness and skill in managing two four-horse wagons.[45] Uncle John liked to say that 'he had gone through the seminary' with Dr Wilson, referring to Wilson's sharing with him at home spiritual truths that he had learned at the seminary.

The 1865 General Assembly adopted a new name—The Presbyterian Church in the United States—and, now that the war was over and the blockade had ended, made plans for its foreign mission work. 'We can scarcely set up a claim to be regarded as a true branch of the Church of Christ, or take an honorable place in the sisterhood of evangelical churches unless to keep this object constantly and distinctly before our minds,' said Dr Wilson. Now in his mid-fifties, Wilson was six feet or more in height, and massive in proportion, 'reminding one of the Doric order of architecture.'[46] The assembly turned the attention of Southern Presbyterians especially to Africa as a field of missionary labor, 'peculiarly appropriate to this Church, and with this view to secure as soon as practicable missionaries from among the African race on this continent who may bear the Gospel of the grace of God to the homes of their ancestors.'[47]

John Leighton Wilson became the missionary voice and conscience of the new Presbyterian denomination, serving as secretary of its Board of Foreign Missions for twenty-five years. In an article for the *Southern Presbyterian Review* he wrote:

> We must rise to those high and clear views of duty that shall make us regard our property, our talents, our

time, and everything else to the great work of regenerating and saving a lost world. And why should we not? It was for this that the Saviour laid down his life. For the same end, the Spirit was promised. For this purpose the church was organized.

Let us all engage in this work more heartily than we have ever done. It is not a hopeless cause in which we have enlisted. We shall not contend as those who beat the air. It is as sure of success, as it is that Jehovah is enthroned in glory; and it is one upon which we shall look back with joy and gratitude, when all the honours, and the wealth, and the pleasures of this world, shall be forgotten.[48]

After the war, home missions included the work of 'sustentation'—helping congregations that had been brokened by the ravages of war, repairing shattered churches, and sending evangelists throughout the wasted land to plant new churches.

Wilson travelled, preached, counseled, encouraged, and exhorted Southern Presbyterians to have hope. He wrote:

A dark cloud hangs upon our horizon, but the great mediatorial King reigns and the church is safe. He who has hitherto defended us from every enemy, upheld us under every trial, and from time to time has bestowed so many precious tokens of his favor upon us as a church, surely will be faithful to the end. Let us then go forward in the path of duty with a firm step and a courageous heart.[49]

In his Harvard dissertation, William Childs Robinson wrote that John Leighton Wilson shone 'with the brightest brilliance' in sustaining and building up 'the torn fragments of the Southern Zion' after the war.[50]

In 1866 the General Assembly of the Southern Presbyterian Church approved a mission to China, and the first missionary sailed in 1867. Within a few years, Southern Presbyterians were serving in Italy, Colombia, Brazil, Mexico, Greece, and Japan. Two men from Columbia Seminary's class of 1869, influenced by the words of Wilson and following the example of Symington, began the Southern Presbyterian mission in Brazil. The longing of Wilson's heart to see a Southern Presbyterian mission to Africa was not to be realized in his lifetime, but in 1890, four years after Wilson's death, Samuel Lapsley and William Sheppard began mission work in the Congo.

The General Assembly sent out a pastoral letter to its churches, exhorting them 'to obey them that have the rule over you' [the reconstruction governments that were being set up] and reminding them of their duty to the African Americans. 'Debtors before to them when bound,' it stated, 'you are still debtors to them free.'[51] The Southern Church's greatest failure came in its treatment of the former slaves. Despite noble aims and ambitions expressed by the pronouncements of its General Assemblies, the church moved slowly and hesitantly in this area and accomplished almost nothing. While treating the African Americans with kindness and respect, John Leighton Wilson, with his great heart and love for Africa and the Africans, might have exerted a more powerful influence. Dr Wilson, wrote Robert Lewis Dabney, 'wielded more real power in the Southern Presbyterian Church than any other man in it.'[52] Rather than lead the church, however, Wilson allowed matters to take their course, which led to greater alienation between white Presbyterians and their former slaves. Wilson loved the black people and he loved the South, but he did not bring them together—and they went their separate ways. It took generations before the Presbyterian Church, and other Southern churches, began to awaken to their failure to stand for black equality in the church and in the culture. Wilson's warning to the South about its guilt in slavery was not repeated in his words about its treatment of the freedmen. He was far from being a racist, but he missed the opportunity to influence his people to do the right thing.

In 1875 the office of Secretary of the Executive Committee on Foreign Missions was moved from Columbia, South Carolina, to Baltimore. The Wilsons lived in Baltimore until 1884, when they went home to Salem in the Black River community in South Carolina. Wilson requested that he be relieved of his office as secretary, writing to the 1885 General Assembly:

> It is not a little gratifying to be permitted to withdraw from this work at a time when it combines within itself all the essential elements of hope and prosperity. The cause of foreign missions now holds no doubtful place in the heart of the Southern Presbyterian Church … The cause has enthroned itself in the affections of the great body of our Christian people to remain there as long as we have any claims to be regarded as a true church of the Lord Jesus Christ.[53]

At home in South Carolina, Dr Wilson planted a garden and experimented with seeds that missionaries sent him from their countries. He did not preach to the white congregation at Mount Zion, but was always ready for service at Mount Sinai, where the black people worshiped. His last sermon—from the words 'Let this mind be in you which was also in Christ Jesus'—was a farewell to his friends at Mount Sinai.

In July 1885 Jane Wilson died, followed almost exactly a year later by her husband. 'Side by side,' Dr and Mrs Wilson 'are sleeping today near the door of the house of God in which his fathers offered worship, the sanctuary among the pine trees known as Mount Zion,' wrote Henry Alexander White.[54] At the opening of the Synod of South Carolina in 1890, a memorial sermon was preached on the life and character of Dr Wilson, from the text Hebrews 7:1—'King of Salem, priest of the Most High God.'

In 1936, John Miller Wells wrote to a number of Southern Presbyterian missionaries and mission leaders to ask what principles they followed in their work. They responded with five: Christ is the head of the church; the preeminent duty of the church in its foreign missions work is the preaching of the gospel; the leadership of the Holy Spirit must be sought and followed; the importance of placing upon the native Christians and church the task of saving their own people and land should be recognized; obedience to Christ's command in foreign missions is the hope for the church itself here at home. Every one of these principles, Wells wrote, was 'held, taught, and used by our first great secretary'—John Leighton Wilson.

> *How beautiful are the feet of those*
> *who preach the good news!*

4

DAVID LIVINGSTONE
(1813–1873)

He was one of those who brought slavery to an end.

IN *The Woman Who Walked in Sunshine*, one of the books in Alexander McCall Smith's *No. 1 Ladies' Dectective Agency* series, Mma Ramotswe is talking with Mr Polopetsi about the practice in modern Africa of changing the names of streets and places from those of the colonial period. She says:

> Some of the people from those very old days had a memory that should be cherished. There was more than one Moffat Road in Botswana, and rightly so, because Robert Moffat had been such a great man. He had been a friend of the Botswana people; he had been the first to put the Setswana language into writing, and he had done so much to help those in need. And then there was Livingstone himself, who had married Moffat's daughter and been attacked by a lion out by Moleopole, not far away.

'He was a very good man,' Mr Polopetsi says. 'You would not want to change anything named after a man like Livingstone. He was a very brave man, Mma Ramotswe. He was one of those who brought slavery to an end.'

David Livingstone's ancestors included Presbyterian Covenanters as well as a great-grandfather who was killed fighting on the Jacobite side at the Battle of Culloden. David's grandfather was born in 1788 on Ulva, a small island off the coast of Mull, close to Iona, an important place for Scottish and Christian history. In 1865 David Livingstone visited Ulva and found the ruins of his grandfather's croft in a green, fertile, but empty place. The failure of the potato crop in the early 1790s caused the six hundred inhabitants of Ulva to leave their island, mostly for the United States and Canada, but David Livingstone's grandfather took his family to Glasgow instead. He carried with him a letter from the kirk on Ulva stating that he had 'always maintained an unblemished moral character, and is known for a man of piety and religion.'[1]

In 1810 David's father, Neil Livingstone, married Agnes Hunter, the daughter of a tailor. David was born in a cotton mill tenement in Blantyre, near Glasgow, on March 19, 1813. He remembered listening as a child 'to his grandfather with delight, for his memory was stored with a never-ending stock of stories,' many of which were like those that David would later hear 'while sitting by the African evening fire.'[2] David's grandmother sang Gaelic lullabies and songs to him and his siblings.

David Livingstone's parents were devout Christians, his father a door-to-door tea salesman who distributed gospel tracts with his tea. David wrote about him:

Though too conscientious ever to become rich as a small tea-dealer, by his kindliness and winning ways he made the heart-strings of his children twine round him as firmly as if he had possessed, and could have bestowed upon them, every worldly advantage. He reared his children in connection with the Kirk of Scotland—a religious establishment which has been an incalculable blessing to that country; but afterwards he left it, and during the last twenty years of his life held the office of deacon of an independent [Congregational] church in Hamilton, and deserved my lasting gratitude and homage for presenting me, from my infancy, with a continuously consistent pious example, the ideal of which is so beautifully and truthfully portrayed in Burns's Cottar's Saturday Night.[3]

From his earliest years, Christian faith and hard work shaped David Livingstone's life. At age nine he could recite from memory all one hundred and seventy-six verses of Psalm 119. When he was ten years old he began to work in the Blantyre Mill. After a twelve-hour day, he attended classes for another two hours, studying Latin, botany, theology, and mathematics. He loved to roam through the beautiful Lanarkshire countryside, where he found shells embedded in stone and collected specimens of plants.

The warm fellowship of the Congregational church where his family worshiped strengthened David's faith and led to his dedication to foreign missions, 'to consecrate my whole life,' he wrote, 'to the advancement of the cause of our blessed Redeemer.'[4] Livingstone studied medicine so that, like Christ, he could both preach and heal. For two years he took classes at Anderson's College in Glasgow, where he 'received a thorough basic scientific training in possibly the liveliest centre of scientific education in the United Kingdom at that time.'[5]

In 1837 Livingstone applied to the London Missionary Society, an interdenominational mission that was then the major missionary organization in the United Kingdom. To meet the mission's requirements he wrote an essay in which he described fallen humanity and God's salvation:

> The Bible treats man as a moral and accountable agent. Salvation is freely offered to him. Believe on the Lord Jesus Christ and thou shalt be saved—faith in the work of Jesus Christ is all that is required to shield him from everlasting punishment. Yet he will not believe it, unless the Holy Spirit exerts his influence over his will by convincing him of sin, showing him the deceitfulness and desperate wickedness of his own heart, the folly and danger of living in sin, and exhibits to his view the beauty of holiness.[6]

The Missionary Society sent Livingstone to London to continue his study of medicine, while he also prepared for ordination. There he met Robert Moffat, a veteran missionary in southern Africa, and his future father-in-law.[7] A Scot, Moffat challenged his young countryman to 'advance to unoccupied ground' in Africa, where, he told him, he 'had sometimes seen, in the morning sun, the smoke of a thousand villages where no missionary had ever been.'[8]

Before leaving for Africa, Livingstone was able to spend only one night with his family in Blantyre. His sister described their parting. 'On the morning of the 17th November [1840], we got up at 5 o'clock. My mother made coffee. David read the 121st and 135th Psalms, and prayed. My father and he walked to Glasgow to catch the Liverpool steamer.'[9]

David Livingstone was ordained in London and, on December 8, departed for Africa. After a rough four-month voyage by way of Brazil he arrived in Cape Town. En route he studied Dutch and Tswana, the language of the people with whom he was to work, and read Charles Bridge's *Reflections on the 119th Psalm*, his heart often warmed by Bridge's 'heavenly-minded reflections.' Livingstone was the only passenger to go ashore in Rio de Janeiro. He explored the city, shared a meal with a peasant family, and ventured into a notorious dockside pub to distribute gospel tracts. His chief friend on the voyage was the captain, who gave Livingstone a thorough training in navigation, a skill that stood him in good stead on one occasion in his life, when he piloted his steamer from the east coast of Africa to India.[10]

David Livingstone spent most of the next thirty-two years of his life in Africa as a missionary and explorer, covering some forty thousand miles on foot, by ox cart, by steamer, or by canoe through uncharted territory, suffering great hardship and much sickness, including twenty-seven bouts of malaria, by one historian's count. Running through all the years of his life, writes Cecil Northcott, was 'the thread of devotion to Africa woven in with his concern that the continent should be Christianized.'[11]

After a month in Cape Town, Livingstone started from Port Elizabeth and made the five-hundred-mile journey by ox cart to Robert Moffat's station at Kuruman, 'an oasis in the wilderness,' where Moffat was working to translate the Bible into the Tswana language. On January 9, 1845, David

Livingstone married the Moffat's daughter Mary.[12] David found Mary to be 'a devout young woman, who could speak Tswana, and knew Africa and how to live in the bush.' Their marriage, Andrew Ross writes, 'was a marriage of love and affection.'[13]

When Livingstone began his treks deeper into Africa, Mary sometimes accompanied him. He needed her and she was dismayed when he left her behind. After an appallingly difficult crossing of the Kalahari in the middle of August in 1850, Mary gave birth to a little girl, Elizabeth, who soon died. David wrote to his father-in-law:

> Have just returned from burying our child. Never conceived before how fast a little stranger can twine round the affections. She was just six weeks old when called away to see the King in his beauty. Yesterday evening the beautifully formed countenance began to set in death. Then at one o'clock she opened her beautiful eyes and screamed with a great effort to make her lungs work, and instantly expired. That scream went to our hearts, and will probably not be forgotten in eternity.[14]

Mary's father continued his close friendship with his son-in-law, but Mrs Moffat was alarmed and angry when David and Mary were getting ready to go north again. She feared that David was putting Mary's life in danger, as well as any child they might have so far from any medical help. Later when Livingstone planned a long journey of several years duration, he sent Mary and their children to Scotland to stay with his family. After he saw them set sail from Cape Town, David wrote to his wife:

How I miss you now, and the dear children! My heart yearns incessantly over you. How many thoughts of the past crowd into my mind! I feel as if I would treat you all much more tenderly and lovingly than ever. You have been a great blessing to me. You attended to my comfort in many ways. May God bless you for all your kindnesses! I see no face now to be compared to that sunburnt one which has so often greeted me with its kind looks. Let us do our duty to our Saviour and we shall meet again. I wish that time were now. I shall never show all my feelings; but I can say truly, my dearest, that I loved you when I married you, and the longer I lived with you, I loved you better.[15]

After his family had departed, David Livingstone left on his long exploratory treks, praying: 'O Jesus, fill me with thy love now, and I beseech thee accept me and use me a little for thy glory. I have done nothing for thee yet, and I would like to do something. O do, do, I beseech thee, accept me and my service and take thou all the glory.'[16]

When living with David's parents did not work out for Mary and the children, they moved to another house in Scotland and then to England. It is not surprising that Mary, who did not always get along with her own parents, had trouble with her husband's parents. The senior Livingstones loved their grandchildren very much and tried, unsuccessfully, to keep in touch with their daughter-in-law. As far as we know, Mary did not reach out to her sister Helen, who lived in the southeast of England and was in a position to help her. It was a difficult time for Mary Livingstone. She became depressed, struggled with debt, and, according to rumours, drank too much. A Quaker family 'opened their hearts and their home among the Lake-land hills to them and saved Mary's sanity,' writes Julie Davidson.[17]

The two-year trip that David planned became four and a half years, before he was at last reunited with his wife in England. She did not seem to resent his long absence, although Julie Davidson believes that 'her mood was bitter and her faith fragile.'[18] She presented to her husband a poem she had written for him. Davidson writes that its sentiments are 'charged with pain and pleading,' but the poem is also filled with joy and hope.[19] The first verse reads:

> A hundred thousand welcomes!
>   How my heart is gushing o'er
> With love and joy and wonder
>   thus to see your face once more.
> How did I live without you
>   these long long years of woe?
> It seems as if 'twould kill me
>   to be parted from you now.[20]

David Livingstone's *Missionary Travels and Researches in South Africa* (over a thousand handwritten pages written in six months) was published and eagerly read by thousands, including Charles Dickens, who, even though he scorned missions and missionaries, wrote, 'I have been following a narrative of great dangers and trials, encountered in a good cause, by as honest and courageous a man as ever lived.'[21] Livingstone lectured to enthusiastic audiences all over England and Scotland, culminating with an address at Cambridge on December 4, 1857. He ended his speech abruptly and shouted: 'I beg to direct your attention to Africa. I go back to Africa to try to make an open path for commerce and Christianity; do you carry out the work which I have begun. I leave it with you.'[22] The response was immediate and impressive. The Universities' Mission to Central Africa was established and supported by Anglicans at Oxford, Cambridge, Dublin, and Durham. The mission was not a great success, but a little later, soon after Livingstone's death, both the Free Church of Scotland and the Church of Scotland began missionary work in Africa.

At a farewell dinner on February 13, 1857, David Livingstone said that his wife was a true African veteran and 'the central spoke in his wheel.'[23] Mary returned with David to Africa, taking six-year-old Oswell, and leaving the three older children with their grandmother and aunts in Scotland. When Mary and David arrived in Africa, she was pregnant and rather than accompanying her husband on his explorations of the Zambesi she had to stay with her parents in Kuruman, where she gave birth to Anna Mary. Separated from David and missing her other children, Mary decided to return to Britain. She stayed there until July 6, 1861, when she began her last journey to her homeland. She had just over nine months to live. Mrs Livingstone died on April 27, 1862, at the age of forty-one, and was buried beneath a baobab tree on the banks of the Zambesi in a destitute region of Mozambique. Her husband wept like a child, and, for the first time in his life, he said, he too was 'willing to die.'[24] The inscription on the monument placed later on Mary's grave reads: 'Here repose the mortal remains of Mary Moffat the beloved wife of Doctor Livingstone in humble hope of a joyful resurrection by our Saviour Jesus Christ.' David wrote, 'She was a good wife, a good mother, and a good but often fearful and dejected Christian.'[25]

After Mary's death, David Livingstone spent some time in England visiting his children, except for Robert, his oldest son, who was in the United States fighting in the Union Army. Livingstone completed his *Narrative of an Expedition to the Zambesi* and returned to Africa. Travelling by way of Bombay to Zanzibar, he arrived on January 28, 1866. He was glad to be 'home' and, with joy and enthusiasm, set out on another long journey into the heart of Africa. He wrote in his journal, 'No doubt much toil is involved but the sweat of one's brow is no longer a curse when one works for God: it proves a tonic to the system, and is actually a blessing.'[26]

The years took their toll on David Livingstone, but he carried on, determined to fight slavery, to seek the elusive source of the Nile, and thereby to provide a way for commerce and Christianity into the heart of Africa. He hoped, he said, that 'when the day of trial comes' he would 'not be found a more sorry soldier than those who serve an earthly sovereign.'[27] The entry in his journal for January 1, 1871, reads, 'O Father! Help me finish the work to thine honour.'[28]

For months no one heard from Livingstone until the Welsh-American journalist Henry Morton Stanley, on behalf of the *New York Herald*, found him in the heart of Tanzania on November 10, 1871, and greeted him with the famous handshake and words, 'Dr Livingstone, I presume?' Stanley said, 'I thank God, Doctor, I have been permitted to see you.' Livingstone answered, 'I feel thankful that I am here to welcome you.'[29] The two men quickly became friends, but Livingstone refused to go home to Britain with Stanley.

A letter, published in the *New York Herald*, contained David Livingstone's famous words about slavery and the slave trade: 'All I can say in my loneliness is may heaven's rich blessing come down on every one—American, English, Turk—who may help to heal this open sore of the world.'[30] In a letter to his daughter Agnes, he wrote, 'No one can estimate the amount of God-pleasing good that will be done, if, by Divine favour, this awful slave-trade, into the midst of which I have come, be abolished. This will be something to have lived for, and the conviction has grown in my mind that it was for this end I have been detained so long.'[31] In his journal he appealed for missionaries to come 'to the real heathen.' (He never used that word in a pejorative sense.) 'You have no idea how brave you are till you try. Leaving the coast tribes, and devoting yourself heartily to the savages, as they are called, you will find, with some drawbacks and wickednesses, a very great deal to admire and love.'[32]

At the age of sixty David Livingstone died in what is now Zambia on May 1, 1873, at four in the morning, kneeling beside the bed with his head in his hands on the pillow. His African friends, Susi and Chuma, former slaves he had freed, buried his heart under a tree, and read the funeral service from the *Book of Common Prayer*. They wrapped the body in calico and dried it in the sun to preserve it for 'Livingstone's last and most unusual African journey.'[33] They carried Livingstone's body over a thousand miles to the Indian Ocean coast, a journey which took over eight months. From there the body of David Livingstone was brought back to England and buried at Westminster Abbey on April 18, 1874. Behind the coffin walked the seventy-nine-year-old Robert Moffat, Livingstone's father-in-law, while the great congregation sang the 'Old Hundredth'—

> Praise God from whom all blessings flow;
>   Praise Him, all creatures here below;
> Praise Him above, ye heavenly host:
>   Praise Father, Son, and Holy Ghost. Amen.

Livingstone's tomb in the centre of the nave of Westminster Abbey bears the inscription: 'Brought by faithful hands over land and sea, David Livingstone: Missionary, Traveller, Philanthropist. For thirty years his life was spent in an unwearied effort to evangelize the native races, to explore the undiscovered secrets and abolish the slave trade. And other sheep I have, which are not of this fold: them also I must bring, and they shall hear my voice; and there shall be one fold and one shepherd.'

David Livingstone's bones were buried in England, but his heart was buried in Africa, where it belonged. In his journal on June 25, 1868, Livingstone had written: 'We came to a grave in the forest; it was a little rounded mound as if the occupant sat in it in the usual native way. A little path showed that it had visitors. This is the sort of grave I should prefer: to lie in the still, still forest.' But it was not to be. Instead, Livingstone's tomb is in a central place in England's most famous church, visited by hundreds of people daily.

A British magazine paid tribute to the famous missionary-explorer with these words:

He needs no epitaph to guard a name
Which men shall prize while worthy work is known;
He lived and died for good—be that his fame:
Let marble crumble: this is LIVING-STONE.[34]

In seven points I will attempt to briefly summarize and evaluate David Livingstone's life and work.

1. *Livingstone was by no means a perfect man.* Sarah Worden, curator of the David Livingstone bicentenary exhibition in the Royal Scottish Museum, says that Livingstone is 'a complex and engaging subject, a fascinating story of a man who seems on the one hand larger than life, determined and driven, but essentially a fallible and vulnerable individual.' Livingstone combined conflicting characteristics. He was stubborn but long-suffering, judgmental but generous, harsh but gentle, proud but humble, reckless but courageous.[35]

Both friends and enemies said that Livingstone could be notoriously stubborn. He wrote to the London Missionary Society that he would try to follow their instructions, adding that he was willing to go anywhere, 'provided it be forward.'[36] And Livingstone believed that he knew better than anyone which way was forward! (A friend commented that 'in an Englishman we might, I think, have called the phase obstinance, but with Livingstone it was Scottishness.'[37]) The LMS eventually chose to cease to support him, because they judged that his work was only remotely connected with preaching the gospel and planting churches, but later viewed him as their most famous missionary.

Livingstone was not blind to his failures. He said that his heart was 'sometimes fearfully guilty of distrust' and he was ashamed to think of it.[38] After an early clash with a fellow missionary, he wrote to the LMS secretary 'to pray for him that he might not take offence so readily and aggressively.'[39] Late in his life he developed more patience and understanding with people who disappointed and angered him. When some of his African helpers abandoned him on one of his last treks, he wrote, 'I did not blame them very severely in my own mind for absconding: they were tired of tramping and so verily am I. Consciousness of my own defects makes me lenient.'[40]

2. *Livingstone loved his wife and children*. Many books about Livingstone fault him for putting his personal ambitions before the welfare of his family. It is true that his undeviating commitment to what he saw as his God-given work created severe trials for his family, but there is abundant evidence that he loved Mary and the children. Julie Davidson, who is quick to point out Livingstone's faults (claiming that Mary and the children 'became expendable to his vision and ambition'), writes about Livingstone's feelings at Mary's death:

> Nobody has ever doubted that Livingstone's grief for Mary was anything but real and terrible … To her father, Robert Moffat, he wrote: 'I loved her when you gave her over to my charge, and the longer I lived with her, the better I liked her.' Mary's tragedy was that he didn't live with her for very long. They had been married eighteen years, but half that time was spent apart.[41]

3. *Livingstone was, above all, a missionary*. Although much of his time and strength were taken up with

exploration, it was exploration with a purpose—not to satisfy his ambition, although this may at times have been a factor, but to promote the glory of God. He did not establish churches and apparently had few converts, but he never ceased to preach the gospel and in other ways bear witness to the Africans that God loved them and that Jesus died for them. Andrew Ross writes that Livingstone spent his life 'travelling ever further to find new peoples and bring them into the orbit of Christian missions; an effort of pathfinding which would lay a trail that future missionaries, European and above all African, would follow.'[42] During his long and arduous journeys Livingstone 'consoled himself by the fact that he was sowing the seeds of the gospel that hopefully would be cultivated and grow to be harvested later.'[43]

When Julie Davidson asked a Zambian village elder 'how today's Zambians viewed the long-dead white man so honoured by their first president, he replied without hesitation. 'A man of God. Zambia is a Christian country because of Dr Livingstone.'[44] Tim Jeal judged that 'Livingstone appears to have failed in all he most wished to achieve ... Undoubtedly Livingstone's greatest sorrow would have been that Africa never became a Christian continent.'[45] When Jeal wrote those words in 1973, there were already many Christians in Africa. Today there are millions more. Philip Jenkins predicts that 'by 2025, Africa and Latin America will vie for the title of the most Christian continent.'[46]

4. *David Livingstone loved Africa and the Africans*. He found it difficult to get along with his European companions,

frequently initiating explosive outbursts on both sides, but, as Julie Davidson writes, his 'diplomatic instincts when negotiating with Africans were almost always right.' She claims that Livingstone's 'greatest strength was his empathy with the heathens [sic] he had come to convert.'[47]

Livingstone's attitude toward the people of Africa contrasted sharply with that of most nineteenth-century Europeans. His 'compassion for the most oppressed Africans was limitless,' says Julie Davidson.[48] The Boer farmers' 'stupid prejudice against colour' and their treatment of the Africans infuriated him, as did British policy in the Cape.[49] He defended the rights of the Xhosa to fight for their land, and justified the 1851 rebellion of the Hottentots. Andrew Walls writes that there is real truth behind the title of one of the popular biographies, *Livingstone the Liberator* by J. I. Macnair. 'If Livingstone was a herald of imperialism, he was more importantly and permanently a herald of African independence.'[50] At the place in northeast Zambia where Livingstone died and where his heart is buried, there is a tall, stone pillar with several inscriptions, including this one added on the centenary of his death: 'After 100 years David Livingstone's spirit and the love of God so animated his friends of all races that they gathered here in Thanksgiving on 1st May 1973, led by Dr Kenneth David Kaunda, President of the Republic of Zambia.' In his speech that day, President Kaunda lauded Livingstone as Africa's 'first freedom fighter.'[51]

Many Europeans in Africa 'showed neither serious interest in nor any sympathetic understanding of African culture.'[52] Livingstone, however, had a growing appreciation for African culture and, as a doctor, respect for African traditional medicine. He was 'a gifted and observant naturalist.'[53] He shed much light on 'the dark continent' in his books, in which he treated geographical, scientific, linguistic, and cultural observation.[54] Cecil Northcott writes: 'He took Africa seriously and treated its people accordingly. Following his footsteps, no one any longer could call Africa a continent of savages, and in his wake followed a volume of goodwill to Africa that would have surpassed all his dreams.'[55] Andrew Walls agrees: 'His life and writings show a respect for Africans and African personality unusual at the time, and his confidence never wavered in African capacities and in the common humanity of African and European.'[56] Karen Carruthers, manager of the David Livingstone Centre in Scotland, says, 'We get a lot of Africans coming here and for them this is genuinely a place of pilgrimage. Quite often they'll burst into tears or sing.'[57]

5. *David Livingstone supported, but also criticized England's role in Africa.* His often repeated goal and strategy linked 'civilization, commerce, and Christianity.' Civilization and commerce, he believed, would bless the Africans and defeat the slave trade, but to Livingstone they were both means to an end. His ultimate purpose was not to make Africa British, but to make it Christian.

6. *David Livingstone hated slavery and the slave trade.* Livingstone met slavery first in South Africa and later, in its Arab and Portuguese form, in East Africa. He drove himself relentlessly to do what he could to destroy what he called 'the open sore of the world.'[58] In the year David Livingstone died, the last slave was sold openly in the Zanzibar market.

'His exposure of the African inland slave trade could well be counted his greatest achievement,' concludes Cecil Northcott.[59]

7. *David Livingstone's example inspired many to serve God in Africa.* Mary Slessor's missionary call to Africa was confirmed by the death of Livingstone in 1873. Young William Henry Sheppard, an African American born in the South during the era of slavery, went to the Congo in 1890 because of the influence of Livingstone. Peter Cameron Scott, founder of the African Inland Mission, was inspired to return to Africa in 1895, when he read the inscription on Livingstone's tomb, 'Other sheep I have which are not of this fold; them also I must bring.' Alexander Mackay became an engineer-missionary to Uganda in 1876, inspired by Livingstone's conviction that missions should transform the material as well as the moral and spiritual aspects of African life.

David Livingstone travelled thousands of miles, often by foot, back and forth across the great continent of Africa, driven by a two-fold ambition—to close the door to slavery and to open the door for the gospel.

> *How beautiful are the feet of those*
> *who preach the good news!*

MARY SLESSOR
(1848–1915)

Mother of all the peoples.

FRANCIS ITA UDOM, who now lives in Scotland, is the great-grandson of an African woman who, as a baby, was rescued by Mary Slessor from burial alongside her dead slave mother. The baby was adopted by Mary and named Annie. Francis was amazed when he saw a ten-pound Scottish banknote with a picture of Mary Slessor, his great-great-grandmother, and a map of Calabar (now Nigeria) showing his own village where Mary had preached and where she had found Annie.[1] After David Livingstone, Mary Slessor is the best-known Scottish missionary. Appointed a vice-consul in Calabar, Mary is believed to be the first woman magistrate in the British Empire.

Mary Slessor was born into a poor family in Aberdeen, Scotland, on December 2, 1848, the second of seven children.[2] Mary's father, a shoemaker and 'decent enough when sober,' moved the family to Dundee in 1857, where they lived in a tiny one-room house, with no water or electricity. Mary's mother was a patient, deeply Christian woman who wanted her sons to become foreign missionaries. At about age eleven, Mary became a 'mill-lassie,' working part time and attending school for the rest of the day. When she was fourteen years old she had become a skilled weaver, working ten hours a day yet making time to go to night school. Encouraged by the example of David Livingstone, who was a weaver himself and largely self-educated, Mary kept a book with her to read whenever she could.

Mary was a tough, street-smart girl, with striking blue eyes, red hair, and a flaming temper. An elderly neighbour took 'the wild lassie in hand and put the fear of God into her,' she said.[3] Near the end of her life Mary Slessor wrote:

> When I was a young girl, I entered into God's great grace, on the experience of His keeping, sanctifying power, and, excepting for a little while when Cheyne and Driver[4] were at their worst in their destructive criticism, that perfect peace and faith has never wavered, and if anyone may testify as to the reality of His presence and power, it is surely this unworthy servant.[5]

Mary was an active Christian, teaching Sunday school and supporting a youth club in her church. She soon had unruly boys and girls helping her with the sick and elderly around them. She was drawn to missionary work—by her mother's influence, the stories of the missions in Christian publications, and the death of David Livingstone in 1873. She was struck by Livingstone's words that accompanied his obituary and seemed addressed especially to her, 'I direct your attention to Africa. Do you carry on the work I have begun. I leave it with you.'[6]

At the age of twenty-eight, Mary Slessor was accepted by her United Presbyterian Church to be a missionary to Calabar in Africa. She signed her farewell letters 'Yours in Royal Service' and sailed on the SS Ethiopia on August 5, 1876. When she saw scores of casks of rum being loaded on the ship, Mary ruefully exclaimed, 'All that rum! And only one missionary!'[7]

The small Presbyterian mission in Calabar comprised both Scottish and Jamaican missionaries. The mission had been founded in 1846 by Hope Masterton Waddell, an Irish clergyman who had served for twenty years in Jamaica, where he met former slaves working in the sugar plantations who told him about their African homeland. He took some converted Jamaicans with him to Calabar and began the work of evangelizing Africans.

Two centuries of slave trade had cheapened human life, divided tribes, and perverted the culture of western Africa. Although the overseas slave trade traffic had ceased, internal slavery continued. In Calabar human sacrifice was practiced, as was the 'poison bean' ordeal, where guilt or innocence was supposedly indicated by the response of an accused person to a poisoned bean. Unwanted babies were thrown into the bush to die. Babies of mothers who had died were buried alive with their mothers. Twin babies were killed and their mothers driven out of the tribe. It was believed that one of each pair of twins was the child of the devil. Since it could not be determined which, both were killed.

Mary had a deep love for African children and, in her thirty-eight years in Calabar, saved the lives of hundreds, including Francis Udom's great-grandmother. She rarely had less than a dozen rescued babies in her huts. She adopted nine of them, including Daniel McArthur Slessor, who wrote in his reminiscences in 1958, 'Ma was the ideal mother; with us she was not the mistress or the missionary worker, she was our mother and the home our family. A happier family I cannot admit existed.'[8] Mary named one of the babies whom she saved from death Janie Annan Slessor, and adopted her. On a visit to Scotland Mary took Janie with her, and the little girl won many hearts. Janie became Mary Slessor's best friend and often her only companion. For years she nursed her 'Ma' when Mary was sick, taught in her schools, helped in her dispensary, walked miles with her to collect abandoned babies, dug latrines, planted gardens, laundered, and cleaned.

Mary said, 'As long as I can nurse a motherless bairn or help to keep peace in a home, or be a mother to my own bairns, I'm to stick to my post.'[9] When tribal leaders in one of the towns where she lived decided to do away with the tradition of killing twins, Mary wept tears of joy and thankfulness. 'It was a glorious day for Calabar,' she said.[10]

Mary was concerned and angered that women suffered so much from men in the African culture. In the margin of one of her Bibles, beside the passage in which the apostle Paul states that wives must be subject to husbands, she scribbled 'Na! na! Paul, laddie! This will no' do!'[11] (Elsewhere in her Bible, however, she praised the apostle, writing, 'Paul, laddie, comes in for applause,' and 'No worldly truck or muck there! Direct on, lad!')[12]

During her entire missionary career, Mary sought to improve the lives of women by providing them with schools and jobs. Her fifty elementary schools were free and open to all, including girls. Her work in vocational education, for woman and men, led to the opening of Calabar's Hope Waddell Training Institute in 1895, still the largest institute of its kind in West Africa.

Mary was often sick with fever, an inescapable consequence of life in Africa. Less than three years after she arrived in Calabar, she seemed to crumple under the strain. Sick and homesick, she wrote, 'I want my home and my mother.' She even missed her work in the factory, 'listening to the music of the shuttles and it is sweet.'[13] She longed for the cold and snow of a Scottish winter. She wrote:

> Oh, the dear homeland, shall I really be there and worship in its churches again! How I long for a wee look at the winter landscape, to feel the cold wind, and see the frost in the cart-ruts, to hear the ring of shoes on the hard frozen ground, to see the glare of the shops, and the hurrying, scurrying crowd, to take a back seat in a church, and hear without a care of my own the congregation's singing, and hear how they preach and pray and rest their souls in the hush and solemnity.[14]

When she was on furlough in Scotland, Mary was shy and nervous when addressing church congregations. She wrote out her sermons, or 'lessons' she called them, because women do not preach 'in our stern Presbyterian church meetings.' One of her lessons, thirty-five handwritten pages, ended with these words:

Thank God! For such men and women here and everywhere, who in the face of scorn and persecution dare to be singular, dare to stand firmly and fearlessly for their Master. Their commission is today what it was yesterday, 'Go ye into all the world and preach the Gospel to every creature.' This command is exceedingly broad: you see it is not 'look at' but 'go into' the world! Then it is '*all* the world,' not the nice easy places only, but the dark places, the distant places. Then 'to every creature.' To the low as well as the high, the poor as well as the rich, the ignorant as well as the learned, the degraded as well as the refined, to those who will mock as well as to those who will receive us, to those who will hate as well as to those who will love us.[15]

The Calabar mission's work was limited to towns near the coast. From the beginning of her time in Africa Mary longed to go to places where no missionary had been. She was routinely discouraged by her Calabar colleagues and by the mission leaders in Scotland, but Mary was determined to go where she thought God was sending her. When it seemed there was no stopping her, Mary was allowed to go deeper into the country.

She was delighted when she was permitted to work as the only missionary in an outstation at Old Town, three miles upriver from the mission headquarters in Duke Town. There she was happy and busy as preacher, teacher, nurse, and social worker.

Mary conquered a fear she had of rivers, important because her travel was often by boat. When troubled by animal noises in the night, she prayed, 'Oh Lord of Daniel, shut their mouths.'[16] Once threatened by a leopard she sang hymns in a loud voice, until the big cat gave up and ran away! 'Her faith was as great as lions,' her adopted son, Daniel, wrote, 'and her courage greater than warriors.'[17]

Mary was well aware of her own shortcomings and sins. In her diaries and letters she wrote about being irritable, short-tempered, and impatient. The margins of her Bible are filled with notes confessing her failures. Next to Psalm 141:3 ('Set a watch, O Lord before my mouth') she wrote, 'I cannot do it.'[18] But she trusted God to do his work through her. 'God and His Word are a living bright reality for sure,' she wrote, 'and the fact that I meet my congregation knowing that it is not me, nor my message, but just that I am in the hand of the Spirit as the channel of communication and that my part is to see that the channel is open and clean.'[19]

Mary lived like the Africans—indeed, like poor Africans. She made her home in an African hut, ate African food, went barefooted like the Africans, and made do with few, if any, modern items. Without a clock, she sometimes tied a rooster to her bed if she needed to get up early! One thing she could not do without—a cup of tea! She watched breathlessly when a package from Scotland was being opened until she saw, to her great relief, that it included a generous supply of tea.

Mary spoke the African languages well. The Efiks said that she was 'blessed with an Efik mouth.' She mastered not only colloquial phrases but also inflections, guttural sounds, and interjections and sarcasms, as well as the quick, characteristic gestures of the people. Mary translated some English hymns into Efik and set them to rousing Scottish tunes such as 'Sweet Rothesay Bay', 'The Rowan Tree', and 'Scots Wha Hae.' The Africans sang them to the accompaniment of a drum or two and as many tambourines as could be found. They came to love this intrepid Scottish woman, calling her *eka kpukpru owo*—'mother of all the peoples.'

When on one of her furloughs Mary decided to stay in Scotland to care for her ailing mother, Mrs Slessor would have none of it. She repeated what she had said earlier when Mary was considering foreign missions, 'You are my child, given to me by God, and I have given you back to Him.'[20] During 1885 Mary's sister, Susan, died, and Mary's mother died on the last day of that year. Mary wrote: 'Heaven is now nearer to me than Scotland.'[21]

Mary Slessor's pioneering spirit took her far into the uncharted interior of the country—from Duke Town to Ekenge in Okoyong and, finally, to Itu in Igboland. The report of the mission board for 1890 stated that Mary ministered among the Okoyong people 'with extraordinary courage and perseverance.' She loved her Okoyong women and found the men 'gentlemanly and gracious.'

In her prime, she went down the bush paths as fast as most Africans. When an ordained missionary came out to take a service for her in a stifling little church, he was exhausted, and ashamed when he discovered that Mary had held twelve services that day and walked over ten miles! Mary's friends in Scotland worried about her. One wrote, 'Do be careful. Do take quinine and sleep under a net and drink filtered water. Don't be so ridiculously unselfish.' 'Since the rains came,' Mary wrote, 'I have been ever so much stronger, and for over two months I have been able to take 7, 8, and 10 hours on end on Sundays going round the villages, 6 to 9 meetings on end in various places.'[22] She pressed on, even when she was sick, sometimes explaining, 'I have not been ill but I have been unwell.'[23]

Mary Slessor had no missionary strategy, no fixed plans, no schedules. She simply relied on the Lord to guide her and to provide for her. 'After all,' she wrote, 'it is not committees and organizations from without that are to bring the revival, and to send the Gospel to the heathen at home and abroad, but the living Spirit of God working from within the heart.'[24]

She was 'not over-enthusiastic about church methods,' and wrote, 'I would not mind cutting the rope and going adrift with my bairns.'[25] The mission board had come to the decision that Mary was free to go and start new stations wherever she and the Africans wanted them, provided that it did not obligate the mission to additional expense. Mary did not worry about money. She believed that God could and would send the necessary funds for her work as easily as he sends a shower of rain.

Mary Slessor's influence continued to grow among the people, and some African leaders and British officials complained that she was only 'a mere woman.' She replied to one African chief that in judging 'the power of the woman, he had clearly forgotten the power of the woman's God.'

Charles Ovens, who arrived from Scotland in 1889 as a 'short-term' missionary to build Mary a much-needed house, stayed on for fourteen years. He came to know Mary well, and she enjoyed working with him, saying on one occasion, 'It is splendid to have people who know your people at home, and who can sympathize with your inclination to shout 'Hallelujah!' sometimes.'[26]

Charles Morrison, a teacher on the mission staff who was eighteen years younger than Mary, asked her to marry him. She agreed, provided that he would join her at Ekenge. The mission board, however, refused to release Charles from his work of training African teachers at Duke Town. Mary was saddened but would not give up her place of work. She wrote to a friend: 'If God does not send him up here then he must do his work and I must do mine where we are placed.'[27] 'I will still try to be grateful, as He knows best. What the Lord ordains is right.'[28] When Charles's health began to fail, he returned to Scotland before moving to North Carolina, where he died. Mary kept two books in which they had signed their names side by side, and she wrote the words: 'When you have a good thing or read a good thing or see a humorous thing and cannot share it, it is worse than bearing a trial alone.'[29]

'Christ was never in a hurry,' Mary Slessor wrote. 'There was no rushing forward, no anticipating, no fretting over what might be. Every day's duties were done as the day brought them and the rest was left to God.'[30] Mary was delighted when she saw people beginning to live in 'God's fashion.' There were groups of people meeting for worship and keeping the Sabbath, even though there was no pastor and no one who could read. A dying woman in one of these villages told her parents and her husband not to grieve for her. 'I have seen Jesus and I want to go to him, and it is He who calls me, and you must learn and come after me.' Mary commented, 'This from a flock without a shepherd! They just meet and sing and pray and separate. But the Spirit is there! And He teacheth savingly.'[31]

Mary wrote to *The Women's Missionary Magazine* about 'our first baptism and our first observance of the feast of love [Lord's Supper]' at one of the churches. 'It was just a day of heaven upon earth, and the crowds outside, as well as the crowd packed within, were as reverent as if it had been a sacrament day in Scotland. The stillness was intense, and all hearts were touched and subdued.'[32]

When the Foreign Missions Committee visited Calabar in 1910, they met a chief who had built a church with his own money. He 'seemed a true gentleman in all his ways,' they reported, 'and yet it is only four or five years since Miss Slessor led him to the Saviour.' The committee attended a service in one of the villages where a congregation of at least seven hundred people were gathered. 'It was difficult to realize that what we saw had taken place within eight years.'[33] Mary was confident that 'the harvest will be gathered, but as yet it is only the seed time.'[34] The harvest came after Mary Slessor's death. As a result of her work and that of others who followed her, Nigeria today has a large and growing Christian church.

Visitors, meeting Mary Slessor 'outside her mud-walled, palm-thatched house,' were intrigued by her language, 'a charming mixture of English, Scotch, and Efik.'[35] A chief sent a message for them to take back to Scotland, 'Tell them in the white man's country that we thank God and them for sending Ma Slessor to bring us the light. But many of our brothers are in darkness. Will they not send more?'[36]

With the establishment of the Niger Coast Protectorate, the British took over the administration of Calabar District. They began to take note of the Scotswoman who lived, dressed, and spoke like an African and who could prevent battles, out-shout chiefs, and stop riots merely by walking into the middle of them. When the British appointed vice-consuls to supervise the running of native courts, they chose Mary for that office among the Okoyong people. The government was only too glad to have a magistrate who needed no interpreter, understood African customs, and had a personal authority greater than anything they had achieved with their soldiers and weapons. Mary paid little attention to all this, but she was the first woman to be appointed to such a post in the whole of the British Empire.

A former Calabar missionary wrote, 'Let no one think that the spiritual adviser was lost in the law-giver. I am safe in saying that in no court of justice in the world was the gospel preached so habitually.'[37] Mary declared, 'To preach the gospel is our *one* aim in all our work.'[38] She wrote, 'For Christ did not send me to baptize, but to preach the good news, and not to preach that in the terms of philosophy in which the crucifixion of Christ cannot be expressed,' and noted its source, 'Paul, laddie, to the Corinthians.'[39]

In her court duties, Mary Slessor was on call twenty-four hours a day—settling disputes, saving twins from death, evangelizing, nursing, and administering justice. Instead of fighting, the tribal chiefs from as far away as a hundred miles began to take disputes to Mary for arbitration. During the hours she sat listening to arguments about witchcraft, wives, divorces, dowries, slaves, livestock, and land, Mary endured by knitting and chewing homemade toffee. She wrote to friends, 'Pray that I may have both patience and tact, and that I may be able to lift the whole question up to a higher than political plane.'[40] Some resented what they saw as Mary's domineering spirit but they did not harm her. This woman must be protected by the spirits, they reasoned, and therefore no one in his right senses would attack her. And no one, in this world of cruelty and killing, ever did.

A visitor from Scotland wrote about Mary Slessor's court, 'At a little table sits the only woman judge in the British Empire.' Her decision, as usual, was 'accompanied with some sound words of Christian counsel, for this court gives an opportunity to dispense both law and gospel.'[41] A British official said, 'I have had a good deal of experience of Nigerian courts of various kinds, but have never met one which better deserves to be called a court of justice than that over which she presided, and it was essential justice unhampered by legal difficulties.'[42]

In one of her reports to the mission board, Mary mentioned the many claims upon her and asked, 'Where is the time and strength for comprehensive work of a more directly evangelistic and teaching type, especially when the station is manned year after year by the magnificent total of one individual?' Once when Mary was busy with humdrum chores, she wrote, 'Not much evangel there? Eh? Well! It is all for His dear sake, as I am His, and all my work is His.'[43] Mary believed that the founding of schools and such things 'can be the means to an end, and by this open door, we can get in the gospel wedge, which *alone* can help or lift up any people.'[44]

Covenant Seminary professor David Jones summed up Mary Slessor's work as 'a vivid illustration of how the kingdom of God is like leaven permeating the whole of life and society.'[45] In 1908 the Nigerian *Government Gazette* wrote of 'the civilizing influence' of the work of 'that admirable lady, Miss Slessor.'[46]

By her correspondence and ministry during furloughs in Scotland Mary sought to awaken the home church to its missionary responsibility. She said that a 'host' of men and women were needed in order to 'take possession' of any new area 'for Christ.' She was disappointed that so few missionaries were being sent out. She wrote, 'Oh Britain, surfeited with privilege! Tired of sabbath and church, would that you could send over to us what you are throwing away!'[47] The problem with the home church, Mary declared, was that it didn't pray enough. 'If we had a praying people we would have a missionary church and a victorious church.'[48] Mary sometimes felt that she was 'dragging a great Church behind her' into Africa.[49]

Mary Slessor pled for consecrated women to help her in Africa. Women, she said, who were not afraid of work or filth of any kind, moral or material; women who could wash a baby and teach a child to wash and comb her hair as well as read and write; women who could take it all to Jesus and thereby get strength to carry on under any circumstances. Men were also needed. Mary said:

> Where are the men! Are there no heroes in the making among us? No hearts beating high with the enthusiasm of the gospel? Men smile nowadays at the old-fashioned idea of sin and hell and broken law and a perishing world, but these made men, men of purpose, of power and achievement, and self-denying devotion to the highest ideals earth has known.[50]

Mary Slessor loved and honoured her Presbyterian church despite its failings and faults. She admired the 'old Calvinistic Christians' who, like her mother, feared 'presumption and felt surer of a Christian who was very conscious of sin.' Mary deplored the 'noise and fuss and sensation and a craving for something new' in the church and worried that 'the old meditative spirit and the old sense of sin seem to be sadly lacking.'[51] In a letter, she mentioned the demise of a Christian periodical, *The Overcomer*. 'It upheld some aspects of the Christian life,' she wrote, 'but to the rank and file of Christians it was too polemical and too academic in its style. I dare not say too doctrinal, for want of that is the fault and lack of the present day preaching and teaching, I think. Doctrine is deprecated, but I'm Scotch, you see, and have had it in my blood to be doctrinal as a foundation for practice.'[52] Mary was deeply thankful for 'real Scottish love, full of pathos and prayer; the dear love inspired in our strong Scots character by the Holy Ghost and moulded by our beloved Presbyterianism of the olden time.'[53]

During her last years in Calabar Mary spent herself in overwhelming work. She was weak and ill, but she would not give up. Sitting down all alone for tea one day, she prayed out loud, 'Thank you, Faither, ye ken I'm tired.'[54] Mary would not go to Scotland and leave her work for good, but she agreed to go to Grand Canary Island for a two-month vacation that a friend of the Foreign Mission Committee paid for. Mary and Janie, Mary's adopted daughter, were amazed by the splendour of their hotel. 'The sunshine and the breezes,' Mary wrote, 'and the blue expanse of ocean, the gardens, and the atmosphere of love make it like a visit to paradise.'[55] She sat and knitted and worked her way through the Bible all day long. It was 'the most wonderful holiday' she ever had.[56]

Looking back over her life as a missionary, Mary Slessor wrote, 'Mine has been such a joyous service. God has been good to me. I cannot thank him enough for the honour He conferred on me when He sent me to the Dark Continent.'[57] As always Mary gave God all the credit for what she had accomplished:

> My life is one daily, hourly record of answered prayer ... for guidance given marvellously, for errors and dangers averted, for enmity to the gospel subdued, for food provided at the exact hour needed, for everything that goes to make up my life and my poor service, I can testify with a full and often wonder-stricken awe that I believe God answers prayer. I know God answers prayer.[58]

Mary went to Duke Town to be admitted as an honorary associate into the Order of St John of Jerusalem with the award of a silver cross. She was embarrassed at the speeches in praise of her work. When she stood to speak she was silent for a time. Then she turned to some young people and spoke to them in Efik before switching to English. As the longest-serving Scottish member of the mission (some Jamaicans had served longer), she said she received the award on its behalf and not for any special work of hers. 'If I have done anything in my life, it has been easy,' she said, 'because the Master has gone before.'[59]

Beside Paul's words to the Corinthians, 'Death is swallowed up in victory,' Mary wrote in her Bible, 'Hallelujah!

What a climax!' The climax came for Mary Slessor on January 13, 1915. A friend heard her say, 'O God, release me.'[60] And He did. Mary once wrote, 'Don't talk about the cold hand of death—it is the hand of Christ.'[61]

A state funeral was held in Duke Town, attended by government officials, missionaries, students, and many others. The mourners at the graveside sang two hymns, 'When the Day of Toil is Done' and 'Asleep in Jesus.' And that brought to its mortal end the dedicated life of a pioneer missionary who served Christ and Africa. The body of Mary Slessor was laid to rest in a cemetery where at one time the corpses of slaves had been buried.

A friend who served with her in Africa wrote: 'Mary Slessor was a whirlwind and an earthquake, and a fire, and a still small voice, all in one.'[62] When they raised the thirteen-foot-high cross of Scottish granite over her grave, Charles Ovens said, 'It'll tak mair than that tae hold doon orr Mary.'[63]

Mary Slessor wrote, 'Just now I am the feet of the Church, as it were, and I am to go with the shoes of Peace.'[64] For many years, she walked muddy paths, scorching sand, and rugged trails to rescue children, help women, administer justice, and bring the gospel and its message of peace to thousands in Africa.

How beautiful are the feet of those
who preach the good news!

6

SAMUEL NORVELL LAPSLEY
(1866–1892)

A little while to sow the seed with weeping.

ONE day in early March of 1890, two young men stood
in Westminster Abbey at the tomb of David Livingstone.
They were deeply moved by 'the blue-stone slab on which
the brass letters inlaid tell that LIVINGSTONE lies beneath.'[1]
They were Americans—Samuel Lapsley from Alabama
and William Sheppard from Virginia. One was black. The
other was white. One was twenty-three years old; the other,
twenty-four. They were on their way to Africa as missionaries of the Southern Presbyterian Church. At its first General
Assembly in 1861, the Southern Church stated its desire to
be 'an eminently missionary church' and, encouraged by
John Leighton Wilson, singled out Africa as its special field
for work. Lapsley and Sheppard had been instructed by the
church's missions committee to go to west central Africa
and 'to ascertain the most eligible site for a new mission
station.'[2]

Samuel Norvell Lapsley was born into a prominent, prosperous Selma, Alabama, home on March 26, 1866, a year after the Civil War ended.[3] His mother, Sara Pratt Lapsley, was the child of a Presbyterian minister whose lineage was drawn from New England and the Georgia Low-country. Samuel's father, Judge James Woods Lapsley, an elder in the First Presbyterian Church of Selma, was the son of a Presbyterian minister. He was descended from Samuel Rutherford, preacher and scholar who was one of Scotland's representatives at the Westminster Assembly. In 1893 Judge Lapsley became the first layman to be elected moderator of the General Assembly of the Southern Presbyterian Church.

Samuel Lapsley was prepared for college by James Waddell, famous educator who preached and taught in the Lapsleys' church in Alabama in 1880 and 1881. Samuel was an outstanding student and excellent musician at the University of Alabama. He studied at Union Theological Seminary in Virginia for a year and then at the newly founded McCormick Seminary in Chicago, where he helped in D. L. Moody's city missions.

Returning to Alabama, Samuel worked among the people of West Anniston, where his brother Robert was pastor of a new church. Robert wrote of Sam's ministry: 'For the first time in the lives of the poor people in that spiritually neglected locality, there came into their homes, ate at their tables, and walked with them on their streets, one who bore the manifest image of the Lord Jesus.' Samuel moved into that community and lived there. Robert remembered what his brother had told him about the remark of a fellow student at McCormick Seminary. When that student was criticized for going to live in the slums of Chicago where he was working in a mission chapel, he replied that 'he had noticed that the Lord Jesus while here among men did not come down from heaven every morning bringing his dinner with him and go back every night.'[4]

William Henry Sheppard was born in Waynesboro, Virginia, in March 1865, a month before the Confederate surrender at Appomattox. His mother, Fannie, registered as a 'dark mulatto,' was born free in 1837. His father, William, was probably born a slave. William was the village barber and sexton for the Presbyterian church in Waynesboro, where the Sheppard family were devout members. Their son wrote that there were 'so many lovely traits' about his parents that he did not know where to begin.[5]

William Sheppard attended Hampton Institute, whose founder, General Samuel Armstrong, was 'a great, tender-hearted father to us all,' said Sheppard.[6] One Sunday afternoon the school's chaplain invited William to go with him to 'a small village of poor coloured people' where he was beginning a Sunday school. That day Sheppard decided that his life work 'was to carry the gospel to poor, destitute and forgotten people.'[7]

William Sheppard was taken under care of presbytery and sent to the Theological Institute at Tuscaloosa, Alabama, founded in 1877 to train black ministers and missionaries. While in the Theological Institute, and for a year after graduating in 1886, Sheppard served the Calvary Presbyterian Church in Montgomery. In 1887 he was ordained as pastor of the Harrison Street Presbyterian Church in Atlanta.

Sheppard applied to the Southern Presbyterian Committee of Foreign Missions for missionary work in Africa. Following the example of Paul and Barnabas in the book of Acts, the committee waited until they found a colleague to go with Sheppard. In 1890 Samuel Lapsley volunteered. He and Sheppard were appointed as 'coequal' missionaries to the Congo Independent State in Africa. They were commissioned together at the First Presbyterian Church in Nashville, Tennessee.

On February 26, 1890, as the *Adriatic* slowly steamed from the pier in New York, Sheppard wrote, 'Our faces were now turned toward Africa, next to the largest continent of the world, the richest, the darkest, and the most neglected.'[8] Lapsley wrote to his mother, reminding her of their singing 'Jesus, Saviour, pilot me' at 'Mr Moody's meeting,' and closing with the comment, 'Well, I must find Sheppard for prayers.'[9] Lapsley was relieved that his black friend and colleague was treated with respect on the ship. After a voyage of eleven days, the two missionaries arrived in Liverpool and went on to London, where they purchased supplies for Africa.

Lapsley wrote about worshiping in the Church of England on their first Sunday in London. The young Americans were welcomed at the meeting of the North London Presbytery, and they went to hear the famous Baptist preacher, C. H. Spurgeon. Lapsley wrote, 'Mr Spurgeon is of medium height, portly, slow almost with age and weight. Deep melodious voice. Bunyanic, homely English (learnt from old Puritan divines).'[10] Lapsley and Sheppard found in English Christians 'a rare acquaintance with the

Bible, letter and spirit, and a delightful acquaintance with the Saviour.'[11]

Samuel Lapsley visited Brussels on the advice of American friends, since he would be working in Belgian territory in Africa. He was surprised to receive an invitation to meet King Leopold. Lapsley wrote, 'I told him my business, whom I represented—the Presbyterian body in the United States—what I meant to do, and our plan of working with a combined white and coloured force.'[12] 'I quite forgot that he was a Catholic or a king,' Lapsley wrote, 'when he spoke with so much apparent sympathy of my mission.'[13] Little did Lapsley know that Leopold was creating a brutal labour camp in his vast territory of Congo that would lead to the mistreatment, torture, and deaths of thousands of Africans.

When Sheppard and Lapsley left England, some fifty Christians 'filled the platform and sang hymns of encouragement.'[14] On the *Afrikaan*, a small Dutch trading ship, the Americans enjoyed pleasant fellowship with fellow passengers, mainly English Baptists and Swedes from the 'new Evangelical Church,' who were also going to Africa as missionaries. The ship reached Congo on May 9, 1890. The two American missionaries travelled inland by boat, the same route taken that month by Joseph Conrad, whose vivid descriptions are found in his novel *Heart of Darkness*.[15] Lapsley was impressed with the African people—'muscular, active, rather slight than big, and with faces I liked to watch.'[16] Sheppard was delighted to be in the land of his ancestors.

For more than a year Lapsley and Sheppard travelled up the Congo River, seeking the best place to locate the

American Presbyterian mission. They visited the American and English Baptist mission stations along the river. One of the Baptist churches had four hundred members, who, Sheppard wrote, 'preach the Lord Jesus Christ beautifully in their lives.'[17] When navigation of the lower river came to an end, the two men trekked two hundred and thirty difficult miles (with a caravan of Africans carrying their goods) to Stanley Pool, where the upper river was reached and navigation was again possible. Then came what was described by Sheppard as 'eight hundred miles of peril'—cataracts, whirlpools, storms, problems with the steamer on which they were travelling, hippopotami and crocodiles in the river, and from time to time threatening natives. Lapsley wrote, 'A lonely place to work this would be but for the belief in the experience of Jesus' presence! I am praying daily for a strong hold on that blessed fact.'[18]

Sheppard and Lapsley began their ministry to the Africans long before they reached Luebo, which became their mission centre. Sheppard described the first service he and Lapsley held in the Congo. 'We pitched our tent near a beautiful cool stream. At nine o'clock the dish pan was beaten and [our] caravan assembled for divine service. Lapsley read Luke 2:1-12 and we sang 'We're Marching to Zion.' One of our carriers offered prayer, then Mr Lapsley and I followed with prayers in English. The natives sang splendidly and heartily.'[19] Samuel Lapsley found that preaching with a translator was 'very unsatisfactory.' It was hard for him to 'keep up steam.' Quickly he learned enough of the native language that he was able to pray with the people and tell them 'in their own language who Jesus is, why he came to this earth, and how he died for sinners. It was the greatest pleasure to see how they listened to the 'old, old story,' which was all new to them.'[20] Lapsley, who had a fine voice, sang to groups of women in the markets, songs such as, 'Wonderful Words of Life' and 'Nothing But the Blood of Jesus.'[21] To his mother Lapsley wrote, 'I am getting impatient to find my own flock, and have a longing to be face to face with my life work. Yet the longer God protracts the preparation, the more my gain.'[22]

The moon and the stars 'shine nowhere so brightly and beautifully as in "Darkest Africa,"' Sheppard wrote.[23] He found hunting 'a pleasant and profitable pastime and a splendid way in which to pick up the native language,' but 'an extremely dangerous one.'[24] After ignoring warnings that he should not go into the river to secure a dead hippopotamus because of the possibility of being caught by crocodiles, Sheppard narrowly escaped. 'Many times in Central Africa,' he wrote, 'foreigners get into serious difficulties from which they cannot extricate themselves by disregarding the advice of natives.'[25] To his father, Lapsley wrote,

> 'Hitherto hath the Lord helped us.' I am very sure, and it gives me good hope that he means for us to do good out here. I am awaiting only the steamer which shall take us up the great river, which we have come to regard quite as our home, though we go like Abraham, 'Not knowing whither we go,' but possessed with a desire for a full occupation of the whole valley and trusting in Him to show the strategic point for us to begin the attack.[26]

As they travelled further into the Congo, Lapsley wrote, on May 5, 1891, 'We are out of the world now, if it is possible to be so in the heart of Africa. I am not lonely, plenty of work, plenty of company, and more of heavenly companionship than I used to enjoy.'[27]

The two Southern Presbyterian missionaries, Samuel Lapsley, the son of a slave owner, and William Henry Sheppard, the son of a slave, loved and admired each other. To his mother Lapsley wrote, 'Sheppard is a most handy fellow and is now a thorough river-man. His temper is bright and even—really a man of unusual graces and strong points of character. I am thankful to God for Sheppard.'[28] To an aunt, Lapsley wrote, 'Sheppard is a treasure.' The Africans think 'there is nobody like "Mundele Ndom," the black white man, as they call Sheppard. I am very happy to think that you pray for him and me both.'[29] Sheppard loved Lapsley as a brother. Later, when Lapsley died, Sheppard went to a quiet spot in the forest to 'pour out [his] soul's great grief to Almighty God.' 'I had nursed Mr Lapsley in all his fevers,' he wrote, 'and he in turn had nursed me; and now the Master … called him, the better prepared of the two, to himself.'[30]

As the missionaries travelled on to reach the Kasai region, where they had decided to locate the Presbyterian mission, Lapsley found himself singing a hymn he had heard in England:

> Wherever He may guide me,
>   no want shall turn me back;
> My Shepherd is beside me,
>   and nothing can I lack.
> His wisdom ever waketh,
>   His eyes are never dim;
> He knows the way He taketh,
>   and I will walk with Him.[31]

Samuel Lapsley wrote about a village they visited, 'These people are, first and foremost, fishermen, and seem a pure and simple race, as fisherfolk should be. Perhaps the Master will have his Peter and James and John from them before long.'[32] Finally the missionaries reached Luebo. Sheppard wrote:

> We pitched our tent in an open space between the forest on the north side of the Lulua river. We could hear the howling of the jackals in the jungle and the hooting of the owls. Mr Lapsley on his couch was sobbing audibly and so was I. So far from home, with thousands of people and yet alone, for not a word of their dialect could we speak. About 5 o'clock in the morning, how our hearts were cheered when we heard the chickens in the town crowing. We laughed heartily and said, 'Well, there is one language we understand, for the roosters crow in the same language as our American roosters.'[33]

A few days later Lapsley wrote, 'Our first Communion Sunday, the second Sunday in our station, is just finished. Sheppard and I have just said "Good-night" after prayer by the supper-table outdoors, and a talk and song.'[34] The missionaries discovered that the people had an idea of God, the creator and preserver of all things, and a tradition that a closer acquaintance with him once existed. After hearing Lapsley preach a sermon on God's love, a woman, who was the leader of the town dances, said, 'If we had known God loved us, we would have been singing to him.'[35] The people loved the Christian hymns, translated by Lapsley into their language. Their favourite was 'We're Marching to Zion.'

The Africans said to him, 'We have not heard this [story of Jesus]. You white people know but we don't.'[36]

Sheppard and Lapsley bought two houses made of thick mats tied to a framework of poles (for 50 cents each in the equivalent of American money), moved them to their land, and planted palms, bananas, plantains, and rows of pineapples around them. In the evenings they took their 'promenade' up and down the walk they built, which they named 'Pennsylvania Avenue.' 'One morning as Mr Lapsley's door blew open a native saw a strange sight,' Sheppard wrote.

> It was Mr Lapsley on his knees by his couch with his face in his Bible, praying. The native was anxious to know of me what it all meant, and so I had the pleasure of explaining to him that Mr Lapsley, their friend, was talking to the Great King above about them. The native was so pleased he ran back to the town and told it to the people. They had never heard of Jesus, never. And there was our Lord and Saviour Jesus Christ, standing in their very midst, upon two bleeding feet, with two hands outstretched, bleeding, to press those millions to a broken heart, and they had never heard of him—never![37]

Lapsley wrote to his brother James, 'I am very well and very happy, except when I let things make me careless about seeking God's help and comfort in prayer. I like the black folks very much. They are not stuck-up, though they are ready to stand up for themselves. They are very funny and lively and make good company.'[38] Sheppard wrote that the Bakuba people of the Kasai were 'dignified, graceful, courageous, honest, with an open, smiling countenance and really hospitable.'[39] He was astounded to find 'a people in Central Africa so intelligent and yet so far from the truth.'[40] The missionaries hated two common African practices— trial by poisoning (it was believed that an innocent person would survive such poisoning) and human sacrifice (to provide nobility with servants and greater prestige in the afterlife). Sheppard wrote that it was 'only by preaching God's word, and having faith, patience, and love will we eradicate the deep-rooted evil.'[41] Lapsley became something of a doctor, learning to treat himself and Sheppard and then the Africans. 'It is always a good means of interesting them in the "Balm of Gilead,"' he wrote. The people sang a song about Lapsley, 'He gives us medicine. Makes us see life.'[42] They were amazed that he did not want to be paid for his services as the witch doctors did.

To live and work in central Africa, missionaries needed permission from the Belgians of King Leopold, who controlled the area. 'It is doubtful whether missionaries get more immediate good than harm from "state protection,"' wrote Lapsley. 'But without the present secular occupation, the missionaries would have been obliged to conquer a foothold inch by inch. The state makes this interior field accessible.'[43] Lapsley and Sheppard tried to make it clear that they did not work for Leopold and the Belgians, who were exploiting the land for ivory and rubber. Lapsley explained to the Africans that 'our business was not to trade, but to teach the will of their King and ours, the God who made us both.'[44] As they settled into life at Luebo, Lapsley was already planning an extension of their ministry. He wrote to his brother James, 'I want to see another station at the mouth of the Sankuru river when our reinforcements come, and our supplies; and from Sankuru mouth would work up that river, placing our next post one hundred miles up, and possibly move [the people] inward toward the capital of the great Bakuba king, Lukenga, some of whose people I have seen trading here.'[45]

Samuel wrote to his mother that he often longed for home but at the same time was 'never homesick. But I think now of two trips, one to you all in a few years, another to a lasting home, which I hope to reach after a good deal of the good work I was sent here for.' In a letter to his father, he wrote, 'I am well and in excellent spirits. I believe the American Presbyterian Congo Mission is going to do good, and I hope to continue to work here "if God wills."'[46] God did not so will, and Samuel Lapsley died on March 26, 1892, only two years after he had arrived in Africa. He had made the long journey back to a town on the coast on mission business. There he became sick with malaria, a disease that threatened him during his entire time in Congo. An account of his last days is given by the Baptist missionaries with whom he was staying. Knowing that this time he would not recover, the twenty-six-year-old Samuel 'gave a few directions about his things; told where his will was to be found; spoke of the prospects of his mission when he should be gone, trusting that God would more than fill his place; and, commending his native lads to [the care of the missionaries with whom he was staying].' He said he was 'going home,' and sent 'good-bye' to all his friends. 'We laid our brother's body to rest on Sunday morning, in our little cemetery among the trees down by the river-side, where sleep quite a number of our brethren "until he come,'" wrote one of the Baptist missionaries who cared for Lapsley during his last days.[47] Another missionary wrote that Samuel Lapsley's death was 'a terrible loss to his mission; for, apart from the courtesy, shrewdness, and tact which distinguished him as specially fit for the delicate and difficult task of starting a mission in such a country [as the interior of the Congo], he had acquired most valuable experience and information, as well as a fair knowledge of the native languages. I earnestly hope that the Presbyterians of the Southern States will support earnestly and vigorously this mission to the Kasai and be in no way discouraged by this terrible loss.'[48]

On May 25, two months after Samuel Lapsley's death, a steamer reached Luebo. When they heard its horn, Sheppard and the Bakuba men, women, and children hurried to the river expecting to meet their friend and welcome him home. The captain handed Sheppard a letter that told of Lapsley's death. The people wept as though one of their own children had died. Lapsley had, in Sheppard's words, 'found his way into their country, their homes, their language, and into their hearts.'[49] The next day Sheppard wrote to Samuel Lapsley's mother a beautiful and moving letter expressing his deep love for her son.[50] It deserves to be quoted in full.

> I know you have wondered why I have not written, or why I was not the first to break to you the sad news; but, as you may know, we were a thousand miles apart. And at this point of the interior we get a steamer once, or perchance twice, a year.
>
> About the first of January your darling son was sick with a fever. In three days he was feeling much better. A steamer—the *Florida*—came in just then.

Mr Lapsley and I both thought that a change for a month or so would be beneficial to him, as he also had some business with the governor about our land. And he thought to accomplish this, and to look after the transport at the same time. So he secured a passage, and left January 6, 1892, for Stanley Pool.

Dear Mrs Lapsley, that Wednesday morning, February 26, 1890, at the foot of W. 10th Street, New York, just a few moments before the *Adriatic* left for England, you placed your arms around your boy, and gave him his last kisses and Godspeed till you should meet again, and turning to me, remarked, 'Sheppard, take care of Sam.' We went at once into Mr Lapsley's cabin and prayed that the good Master would comfort you and protect us. We held daily communion with God. We spent a month in England, being together always. On board the steamer *Africaan* we held daily private prayer, and would often mention and ask special blessings upon our parents, whom we were leaving. We entered Africa and proceeded as we procured information. We have never been separated for any length of time since we left America. I can place my hand on my heart and look straight up to God and say conscientiously I have kept the charge you gave me. I have loved and cared for him as if he were my own brother. The last words of one of his sisters at the depot in Anniston was, 'Sheppard take care of Sam.' It has not only been a duty of mine, but a pleasure. I have nursed and cared for him in all his sickness. And he has done the same for me. When I have been sick his eyes knew no sleep. By my side he would sit and give medicines. On our canoe trip up the Kasai he was quite sick with hematuric fever. It was the rainy season, and we were unduly exposed. So we camped for three days on a beautiful island near the Kwango. There was nothing that we could get that was nourishing for him. And he remarked, 'Oh! I wish my dear mother was here. She would know just what to do for me!' Shortly after this trip we came to Luebo, and here we have laboured as best we could in promoting the Lord's kingdom. Every day we would have prayer, and lecture with our people. Not only has he been zealous to tell the natives of Christ, but the French traders also. Many nights, when all were wrapt in sleep, he would be walking up and down the walk, communing with God.

Yesterday, May the 25th, when the steamer blew, I at once ordered the people to sweep the walks and fix everything, so that the station would present a nice appearance. I hurried to the river and crossed in a canoe to meet him and bring him home. I entered the steamer and asked for Mr Lapsley. The captain informed me that he had not come, and at the same time, handed me a handful of mail; so I hurried and opened a letter to get some news, and oh, how sad the news! I was struck dumb. The letter read thus: 'Your friend and brother has joined the faithful of all ages.' He who left me a few months ago, and said, 'Goodbye Sheppard; God bless you; I will return by the next steamer,' dead? Oh! is it possible? He, my comrade and co-worker, from whom I have not been separated these two years, now dead? ... It was sad. Oh! more than sad. And the men, women, and children weeping for him they loved. And today (the 26th) they have been crowding in and asking is the news true? The greatest weepers were the chief's family, whose son was Mr Lapsley's personal boy.

My dear Mrs Lapsley, what am I to do? My friend and brother has gone to be with Christ, and I shall see him no more. No more kneeling together in prayer! No more planning together future work! His work is done, and he is now blest with peaceful rest. Oh, that I could have nursed him, that I could have kneeled at his bedside, and heard his last whispers of mother, home, and friends. This is my sorrow that I was not by his side while he fell asleep. I know that your heart is breaking. I wish I could say a word to comfort you. Little did you know that his farewell was forever. But he shall be standing at the beautiful gate waiting for us. We shall soon join him, where farewells and adieus are sounds unknown. We will submit to the Master's will, saying 'Not ours but thine be done. What I do thou knowest not now, but thou will know hereafter.'

Sleep on, beloved, sleep, and take thy rest;
Lay down thy head upon thy Saviour's breast;
We love thee well, but Jesus loves thee best.

Humbly and obediently,

Sheppard

Robert Lapsley recalled that his 'most vivid and precious memory' of his brother was that of his face and words as he played and sang the hymn 'Oh, for the Peace that Floweth as a River.' 'He would say,' wrote Robert, 'and we now see it was prophetic, "This always carries me forward to the Congo."'[51]

Oh, for the peace that floweth as a river!
Making life's desert places bloom and smile,
Oh, for the faith to grasp heav'n's bright hereafter,
Amid the shadows of earth's 'little while.'

'A little while' for patient vigil keeping,
To face the storms and wrestle with the strong,
'A little while' to sow the seed with weeping,
Then bind the sheaves and sing the harvest song.

'A little while' the earthen pitcher taking,
To wayside brooks, from far-off fountains fed,
Then the parched lips its thirst forever slaking,
Beside the fullness of the fountainhead.[52]

William Sheppard described how Samuel Lapsley had come back from a missionary journey

tired, worn, and weary, and walking with a limp. He had been scorched by the sun, beaten by the rains, and torn by thorns; his coat was in tatters, and his last pair of shoes worn into holes; but through all of this he had that heaven-born smile as he said, 'Sheppard, how are you? I am glad to see you.' I could not refrain from withdrawing to the bushes nearby, and there in the quiet I thought of the beautiful Southern home on the hillside in Anniston, Alabama, of the clothing, food and comfort in that home, of the dear hearts of that home who so loved Mr Lapsley, and I broke down in spirit and wept.[53]

*How beautiful are the feet of those
who preach the good news!*

7

WILLIAM HENRY SHEPPARD
(1865–1927)
and
LUCY GANTT SHEPPARD
(1867–1940)

Shepherd and shepherdess of his sheep.

JESUS said, 'If anyone would come after me, let him deny himself and take up his cross daily and follow me' (Luke 9:23). William Henry Sheppard took up his cross and followed Jesus into the heart of Africa. He wrote about it in a poem.

> God laid upon my back a grievous load,
> A heavy cross to bear along the road;
> I staggered on, till lo! One weary day,
> An angry lion leaped across my way.
> I prayed to God, and swift at His command
> The cross became a weapon in my hand;

It slew my raging enemy, and then
It leaped upon my back a cross again!

I faltered many a league, until at length,
Groaning, I fell and found no further strength.
I cried, 'Oh God! I am so weak and lame,'
And swift the cross a winged staff became.
It swept me on until I retrieved my loss,
Then leaped upon my back again a cross.

I reached a desert; on its burning track
I still perceived the cross upon my back.
No shade was there, and in the burning sun
I sank me down, and thought my day was done;
But God's grace works many a sweet surprise.
The cross became a tree before mine eyes.
I slept, awoke, and had the strength of ten,
Then felt the cross upon my back again.

And thus through all my days, from that to this,
The cross, my burden, has become my bliss;
Nor shall I ever lay my burden down,
For God shall one day make my cross a crown.[1]

After the death of Samuel Lapsley in 1892, William
Henry Sheppard, was left to carry on—and he did so admir-
ably.[2] His impressive bearing and linguistic ability gave him
a hearing when he told the people of the Congo 'the new
and wonderful story of Jesus.' His geographical discover-
ies and study of African culture and art were followed
with interest in England and America. On June 23, 1893,
the Royal Geographic Society elected the twenty-eight-
year-old Southern Presbyterian missionary a fellow, one of
the youngest members ever inducted into the society. He

succeeded in his long battle to expose the atrocities carried out by the Belgians of King Leopold in the Congo. He saw a great church growing from his and Lapsley's faith and works.

Henry Sheppard was a radiant and optimistic missionary. He experienced trials and discouragements, but he knew, as he wrote in his poem, that 'God's grace works many a sweet surprise.' One of those sweet surprises came soon. Some weeks after receiving the news of Samuel Lapsley's death, William Sheppard made a journey to the region of the Bakuba people where Lapsley had hoped to plant a church. The king sent word to Sheppard that he could not enter his country. Sheppard replied, 'Mr Lapsley, your friend and mine, desired so much to journey into [this] land, and it was his purpose to take this trip, but you have the sad news that he will journey no more with us.' The king relented and Sheppard cautiously made his way into what he called 'the forbidden land.' He prayed, 'O Master, thou who art everywhere and who hast all power, govern the heart of King Lukenga, and may there be opened a road for thy gospel into the very heart of this dark land.'[3] When Sheppard met the king, he was surprised at his warm reception. The king had decided that Sheppard was one of their tribe and had once lived with them. Sheppard told the king that he was not a Bakuba and had never been to this place before. 'The king leaned over the arm of his great chair and said with satisfaction, "You don't know it, but you are one of the family."'[4] That night Sheppard was invited to hear the king's many wives sing him to sleep. He wrote, 'The thought that brought me to tears was, would these people here and at Luebo, and the thousands between, ever gather in groups for singing to our King and adore him in family prayer?'[5]

In 1894 William Sheppard returned to America for a well-deserved year's furlough, and, he said, 'to marry a very sweet Christian woman.' On his way home he stopped in London, where he met Queen Victoria, gave a speech in Exeter Hall, and displayed the African artwork he had brought with him. In the United States he called on President Grover Cleveland and moved audiences with the story of his and Lapsley's journey into the heart of the Congo. A Southern Presbyterian pamphlet reported that 'Dr Sheppard told the story of his experience [in Africa] in numerous churches and before church assemblies so vividly and so appealingly that the whole Church took the Congo Mission to its heart.'[6]

The 'very sweet Christian woman' who became Mrs Sheppard was Lucy Gantt.[7] Lucy was born in Tuscaloosa, Alabama, on February 21, 1867, to former slave Eliza Gantt, whose husband had deserted her. Eliza had never gone to school but she possessed

> a library of sixty-seven books which she had tried to master, and which, in turn, had mastered her and had shaped the destiny of her soul. The first was *Webster's Blue-Back Speller*, every word of which she had memorized in moments snatched from her multitudinous duties as a slave maid to a Southern society belle and as a helper to her own mother. The other sixty-six books gracing her bare pine table began with *Genesis* and ended with the *Revelation*. With these as texts and the Spirit of God as her teacher, Eliza was prepared to rear her daughter in the nurture and admonition of the Lord.[8]

When she was eleven years old, Lucy Gantt entered Talladega College, a school for African Americans founded by the Congregational Church, where she studied for nine years. Lucy, the youngest student in the school, lived with forty-year-old Maria Fearing, a member of the staff and also the oldest student. 'The little girl without brothers or sisters, deserted by her father, and separated from her beloved mother, found in this rare spirit, and in this mature Christian woman, all that her heart craved.'[9] Lucy graduated from Talladega College in 1886, spent several summers in missionary work among children in Alabama, and for six years taught in a Birmingham city school. During a visit to Tuscaloosa, Lucy met William Sheppard, who was a theological student there. They quickly fell in love, but postponed marriage because William was leaving soon to go to Africa as a missionary. 'Years of hazardous living lay before him; years of waiting and working lay before her.'[10] They corresponded regularly; it took as long as nine months for their letters to reach each other. Lucy toured for a year with the Loudin Jubilee Singers, introducing Negro spirituals to the Northern states and promoting the cause of education for African Americans in the South.[11]

In the spring of 1893 Lucy received a telegram from her fiancé saying that he was in London on his way home to the United States. On February 21, 1894, the bride's birthday, William and Lucy were married at the Laura Street Presbyterian Church in Jacksonville, Florida, where Lucy's mother now lived. William arrived the day before the wedding and lost no time in visiting a school for black children and telling them about his life in Africa. This he did in the third person, and ended by saying, 'The man who did these things is to be married tomorrow right here in Jacksonville.'[12] Members of the church decorated their sanctuary with a wreath and bouquets of fresh orange blossoms. When Sheppard and his bride in white walked down the aisle, a whisper swept through the congregation, especially from the children who had heard his story the day before.

William and Lucy Sheppard recruited three African Americans to join them in the Congo mission—Maria Fearing, Lillian Thomas, and Henry Hawkins. The Committee of Foreign Missions did not think it wise to accept Maria Fearing, a fifty-six-year-old woman with less than a high school education. However, with the help of Judge Lapsley, Samuel Lapsley's father, and the women of the Congregational church in Talladega, Alabama, she raised the money for her expenses. The committee conceded and before long instated her as a regular missionary with the usual salary. The committee wrote of Maria Fearing: 'In all the annals of our missionary history there has been no more remarkable and touching instance of consecration to the Master's service than has been recently manifested in the case of a coloured woman in Alabama, who is now on her way to join the Congo Mission. Her plea to be sent to Africa, or to simply be allowed to go, is a touching one in its simplicity and modesty, and indicates the humility and the sincerity of her character.'[13] Lillian Thomas was a student at Talladega College, where Miss Fearing was assistant matron. Miss Thomas and Miss Fearing worked together in Africa and 'their friendship, love, and devotion for each other were akin to that of Ruth and Naomi.'[14] Henry Hawkins was a graduate from the seminary in Tuscaloosa where William Henry Sheppard had studied. In time a dozen African Americans, six women and six men, nearly all recruited by the Sheppards, served with the Southern Presbyterian mission in Congo.[15]

On May 26, 1894, Lucy and William and their three missionary colleagues sailed from New York for England.[16] In London they visited David Livingstone's tomb in Westminster Abbey, as Lapsley and Sheppard had done four years earlier, heard a children's choir sing in St Paul's Cathedral, worshiped at Spurgeon's Tabernacle, and enjoyed the flower-laden air of Hampton Court in the springtime. After a rough voyage on to Africa, the Americans were happy to see, a hundred miles before entering the river's mouth, brown water from the Congo. Lucy eloquently described the river as 'a symbol of the people whose bodies reflected its deep, dark sheen; whose souls had been unfathomable as its depths; whose struggles for centuries had been as varied and as consuming as its rush to the sea; and whose future still remained as unknown as the depths of the river's bed in its whirlpool regions.'[17] The missionaries travelled by foot and by river for a thousand miles to their mission station at Luebo in the Kasai. Tired and bedraggled, they finally arrived in the tropical October moonlight, and for Lucy and William the 'honeymoon voyage of ten thousand miles was over.'[18]

Lucy Sheppard made her home lovely and welcoming. She wrote: 'The making of a Christian home was part of my missionary task and I was glad that my house could be used as a demonstration and practice centre. I called it "The

Ladies' Home Journal House," because so many of the ideas for making furniture and for simple colourful decorations came from that magazine.'[19] Mrs Sheppard plunged into mission work with her husband, even though he tried to convince her not to do so much. He wrote, 'I have found out a few things since marrying—when women set their heads to a good work, they are not easily dissuaded.'[20] A trained teacher, Lucy ran the school. It had no building and no supplies, but there were pupils—mostly slave children redeemed by the missionaries for salt, sea shells, and cloth. From necessity, Lucy became a practical nurse with a make-shift hospital. In 1895, Lukusa, a boy about twelve years old, professed faith in Christ and became the first member of the Luebo Presbyterian Church. Then in quick succession followed six other boys. 'There was joy in the presence of the angels, and who rejoiced even more than the sainted Mr Lapsley,' wrote Sheppard.[21]

Lucy's and William's first baby, Miriam, lived only a few weeks, and was buried beneath a tall palm tree in a little bamboo coffin covered and lined with her mother's wedding dress. Their second child, Lucille, lived eight months. This time there was no wedding dress to line the little box, but native hands placed tropical flowers on the grave, and loving hearts grieved with the stricken parents. Seven months after Lucille's death, on the anniversary of the birth of Miriam, a third daughter, Wilhelmina, was born. Because of Lucy's exhaustion from work and child-birth and the unsettled and dangerous political situation around Luebo, her colleagues advised that she and her baby return to America for a time. From hammock, to riverboat, to ocean steamer, to railroad coaches—through Africa, Belgium, and England—Wilhelmina and her mother travelled safely to America. Lucy and Wilhelmina lived in Virginia with William's relatives.

Mrs Sheppard compiled and published a hymnbook, *Musambu ws Nzambi* (*Songs of God*). It was the first book ever made in the Tshiluba language. In 1899, after a year at home, Lucy returned to Africa, leaving Wilhelmina in Virginia with William's sister and her family. Hundreds of people gathered to welcome her. She learned another language, set up another school, and began the first 'Woman's Society' in the Congo. Working 'cautiously, quietly, but surely,' she began to reach and teach women. She wrote, 'I invited a few to meet with me in my home for a prayer service. Fifty have been coming and we have emerged into a missionary society whose aim is to care for the sick, look up indifferent church members, and help others in need. We are learning to pray and to sing together.'[22] Another child, named William Lapsley, was born to the Sheppards. The little boy was known as 'the speaker of the house,' because he was accustomed to shouting orders![23] The Africans called him 'Maxamalinge,' the name of the son of one of Congo's kings and a friend of Mr Sheppard's. He soon became 'Max.'

In 1897 thirty-year-old William Morrison, a white man, joined Sheppard and his black team in Africa. Morrison grew up in the Shenandoah Valley near Lexington, Virginia, in the home of devout Southern Presbyterians in which blacks were respected. He graduated from Washington and Lee College and from the Presbyterian Theological Seminary in Louisville. Arriving in Luebo sick with fever, he was carried to the Sheppards' home. He wrote to friends in America: 'Mr and Mrs Sheppard have been mine hosts, and most royally do they entertain—generous, refined, kind—a typical home, even if it is in Africa where it is no small task to have a real home.' After observing Sheppard leading a church service, Morrison wrote, 'Whenever he lifts his hand there is silence, whenever he speaks there is closest attention—he is a chief, a prince, an apostle among this people.' Together the two missionaries toured the Kasai, preaching, teaching, caring for the sick, and ransoming slaves. James H. Smylie writes, 'Sheppard and Morrison symbolized a desegregated mission in a segregated church.'[24]

In Ibanche, a village near Luebo, Lapsley Chapel, seating two hundred and fifty, was replaced by a much more durable clay building seating four hundred. Soon another building was needed to accommodate a thousand people. Native preachers, trained in the mission schools, planted 'flourishing churches and schools far away in the interior,' Sheppard happily reported.[25] Southern Presbyterian mission policy declared that native churches 'have the inherent right of self-government.'[26] Scholars of the Hoover Institution at Stanford University wrote in 1966 that William Henry Sheppard 'had the satisfaction of seeing the mission he had founded attracting converts by the hundreds and growing and expanding until it was one of the most important centres of Christianity and civilization in Central Africa.'[27] Before many years the largest congregation of the Southern Presbyterian Church was not in the American South but in central Africa.

By the turn of the century, Belgians were despoiling the Congo, chopping down forests and burning villages to reach and obtain valuable rubber. They recruited an African tribe, the Zappo-Zaps, to enforce their policies. Hardened by years of slave trading and armed with European rifles, the Zappo-Zaps forced people to pay a 'tax' of rubber, food, and slaves to the Congo Free State government and its rubber companies. William Morrison began speaking out about these practices and, with Sheppard's help, organized what became an international human rights campaign. Sheppard collected evidence of the atrocities, documented with photographs from his newly acquired Kodak box camera. The Zappo-Zaps severed the hands of those who failed to produce a required quota of rubber. At one place Sheppard counted and photographed a pile of eighty-one right hands. The 1903 General Assembly of the Southern Presbyterian Church heard Morrison speak. He had come to the United States to plead for the 'emancipation of the Congolese,' and the Assembly voted to send a delegation to President Theodore Roosevelt requesting that the United States intervene on behalf of the people of the Congo.

In 1904 Lucy and William Sheppard came home for a long furlough—his first in a decade. They were reunited with their six-year-old daughter, Wilhelmina, in Virginia. She spoke no Tshiluban and Max, her brother, knew only a few words of English. Their parents translated for them. Sheppard travelled widely, speaking and informing churches and colleges about the Congo. Pagan Kennedy writes: 'On a gruelling trudge through the West and South, [Sheppard] gave a lecture at least every day. He zigzagged from threadbare black colleges in the Deep South to frontier churches in Wyoming, from Ivy League universities like Princeton to a student conference in Nashville where thousands came to hear him.'[28] Dr S. H. Chester, Secretary of Foreign Missions of the Southern Presbyterian Church, presented William Henry Sheppard to a congregation with these words:

> It is my privilege to introduce to you today perhaps the most distinguished and certainly the most widely known minister of our Southern Presbyterian Church. For one thing, he is the only minister on our role holding a fellowship in the Royal Geographical Society of London. On behalf of the Executive Committee of Foreign Missions, I wish to say that there is no missionary on our roll more beloved or more highly esteemed by the Committee under which he serves. During the time of his missionary service he has been called to represent us on many important occasions. He has stood before kings, both white kings and black kings, as our representative. He has never represented us anywhere that we have not had reason to be proud of the manner in which he has done it. He is now recognized both in London and Brussels as one of the greatest of African missionaries. That for which the Committee of Foreign Missions esteems him most is not the fact that he has achieved this prominence and recognition, but that, having achieved it, he has come back to us the same simple-hearted, humble, earnest Christian man that he was when we first sent him out.[29]

In 1906 the Sheppards said good-bye to both their children and returned to Africa, and to a new home at Ibanche in Bakuba territory. 'They were no longer raw recruits, learning new languages and beginning new work in new places. They were now proved veterans, wounded in the fight, but returning to the front from sheer love of hard places and challenging opportunities.'[30] A visitor to the Congo in 1909 wrote that she never met happier, more contented and high-spirited people than the missionaries at Luebo, the principal station of the Presbyterian mission.[31] The missionaries were busy with daily prayer meetings (beginning with morning prayers at 5:45), school for 400 children, catechumen's class, and afternoon service and sermons in the church, plus evening gatherings for prayer and planning.

Oppression of the Africans by the Belgians worsened. Catholic missionaries and some Protestants chose not to get involved, but Southern Presbyterians refused to ignore the colonial practices carried out in greedy pursuit of quick profit. The 1906 Southern Presbyterian General Assembly protested against 'the cruelty and atrocities which have been committed by the military authorities of the government of the Congo Independent State,' and petitioned the American government to 'compel the abatement of this outrage against our common humanity.'[32] The aged and ailing Mark Twain became interested in the campaign of Sheppard's and Morrison's against Leopold's exploitation of the Congo. In one of his last writings, *King Leopold's Soliloquy*, Twain portrayed the king's futile efforts to hide the grim truth. In his 'soliloquy,' Leopold complains about 'the meddlesome missionary spying around—Rev. W. H. Sheppard.'[33] The Kasai Rubber Company brought charges against Morrison and Sheppard for 'tarnishing the honour-ability' of its enterprise.[34] Presbyterian congregations in the

American South set aside May 23, 1909, for special prayer for their accused missionaries, asking 'for their deliverance from any miscarriage of justice under the forms of law, and also for the deliverance of the people of the Congo Independent State from the hand of the oppressor.'[35]

The trial of Sheppard and Morrison was held in Leopoldville in September 1909. The day after Sheppard left for the trial his wife became seriously ill with fever and nervous strain. 'I could not allow myself to think,' she wrote; 'my husband, held by his enemies, my two children in Virginia, and my mother in New Jersey—all separated from me by thousands of miles. I felt the presence of His everlasting arms, and I was comforted by the words, "Lo, I am with you always."'[36]

One side of the courtroom was filled with Protestant missionaries from various denominations and other supporters of Sheppard and Morrison, including two diplomats sent by President Howard Taft, who had said that the United States would follow the trial with 'no little concern.'[37] On the other side were Catholic missionaries, Belgian officials, and supporters of the Kasai Company. Charges against Morrison were dropped because of a legal technicality, leaving Sheppard as the sole defendant. When all witnesses were heard, the judge ruled that the charges against Sheppard be dismissed and that the Kasai Company be required to pay the cost of the trial. On October 4, 1909, the day of his acquittal, Sheppard expressed gratitude to all who had banded together to break the Congolese 'fetters.' He praised those in the American government who 'fought for justice,' those in various Christian denominations who took the 'deepest interest in us possible,' and especially the Southern Presbyterian Church, whose 'holy and high mission has always been to feed the hungry, clothe the naked, and to succour the distressed.'[38] Lucy Sheppard and Bertha Morrison in Luebo fasted and prayed, and 'waited almost breathlessly for the return of [their] loved ones. As the *Lapsley* came steaming in, hundreds of Christians began singing hymns and waving their hands and shouting for joy.'[39]

The headline of the *Boston Herald* celebrated Sheppard's victory—'American Negro Hero of Congo, Was First to Inform World of Congo Abuses.'[40] When Morrison wrote to Sir Arthur Conan Doyle about the trial, the creator of Sherlock Holmes answered, commending Morrison 'for telling the truth about the scoundrels.' In his book *The Crime of the Congo*, Conan Doyle suggested that the trial would make 'a finer Statue of Liberty' than the one in New York Harbour After more than four decades as a cunning and ruthless despot, Leopold became such an embarrassment to his own people that they took his Congo possession away from him a year before he died.

Two months after the trial, William and Lucy decided to leave Africa permanently. The reasons they gave were his ill health and their concern for their two children. A sad, unstated reason was William's adultery with a Congolese woman. Arriving in the United States, William went to Montreat, North Carolina, to meet with the mission committee and make a personal confession. When his wife had been away from him for about two years, he said, he had sexual relations twice with one of the native women.

The committee secretary wrote to Morrison: 'We were all in tears … the confession will bring peace, I believe. "He that covereth his sin shall not prosper, but he that confesseth his sin shall find mercy" … In a short time, with these confessions, the wound will heal. Sheppard can then go to work for the Lord here at home. Only a few need to know about the trouble at all. My heart goes out to him.' Sheppard told his presbytery: 'For the sin which I do confess I have asked God's forgiveness, and have written to the native church at Ibanji, asking its forgiveness. I ask my brethren of the Presbytery of Atlanta also to forgive me for the reproach I have thus brought upon the presbytery as one of its members, and then to impose upon me such ecclesiastical censure as, in its judgment, the honour of Christ and the good of His cause may require.'[42] The presbytery resolved that Sheppard be suspended from exercising his ministerial office for a year. At the end of the year, Sheppard confessed that he had not given a full account of his adultery. He told the presbytery that during his last four years in Africa he 'fell into sin with three different women' on three separate occasions. One of the women gave birth to a son, called 'Shepete' by the Congolese—their name for Sheppard. The boy grew up to take charge of the mission's J. Leighton Wilson Printing Press.[43] While following its disciplinary standards, the Southern Presbyterian Church treated its most famous missionary with kindness and respect. It is possible only to imagine all of Lucy's feelings, but, given her Christian faith, her love for William, and her generous spirit, one can believe that she forgave her husband and encouraged and blessed him. They spent the rest of their lives together working closely in shared ministry.

The presbytery extended Sheppard's suspension a few more months, until April 18, 1912, when he was examined and restored. The Rev. John Little—like Samuel Lapsley an Alabama slave owner's son and a graduate of the University of Alabama—invited William Sheppard to work with him among the African Americans in Louisville, Kentucky. John Little found it distressing that Southern Presbyterians were more interested in supporting missions in Africa than they were in reaching out to the African Americans in their midst. When Grace Presbyterian Church was organized on September 15, 1912, Sheppard became its pastor. It was a tragic time for blacks in the United States. They were increasingly disenfranchised politically, racial separation was becoming more rigid, and the revived Ku Klux Klan and other hate groups stirred up race riots in cities across the nation.

It was a difficult time for the Sheppards. They lived at first in a little house in a crowded, dirty neighbourhood, but they gave themselves to suffering people in Louisville as they had to their people in Africa. Lucy wrote, 'The needs of my race in the homeland were fundamentally the same as they were in faraway Africa, for the longings and the problems of the human heart are alike everywhere.'[44] Both Lucy's mother and William's mother came to live with them in Louisville. Besides caring for her home and family, Lucy Sheppard was busy as a minister's wife, teaching in the Sunday school, training the church choirs, and speaking in churches about the Presbyterian Congo Mission. William Sheppard told about his life in Africa, especially his early adventures with Samuel Lapsley. He enjoyed talking to children, and was known as 'the children's friend.' Sheppard concluded his *Presbyterian Pioneers in Congo*, published in about 1917, with 'the present view.' There were almost 16,000 church members, 160 ministers in training, over 300 Sunday schools, with over 30,000 scholars, and a thousand native teachers. Sheppard wrote, 'When the big bells at the Central Mission stations ring out their inviting peals you can see hundreds of natives with their wives and children, hymn-book and Bible under their arms, wending their way to the house of God. No tongue can tell the great work that God has wrought through the Southern Presbyterian Church for these people, who only yesterday were in darkness and death.'[45]

William Sheppard suffered a paralyzing stroke in 1926. He was sixty-one years old, and died a year later. He laid his burden down, and, as he wrote in his poem, God made his cross a crown. A crowd of more than a thousand black and white people attended his funeral at the Second Presbyterian Church in Louisville, with several hundred more unable to get into the building. He was buried on a hill in Louisville Cemetery. A little later a memorial service for William Henry Sheppard was held at the First Presbyterian Church in Waynesboro, Virginia. One of the speakers, Samuel Lapsley's brother Robert, spoke of Sheppard's ability as a missionary and minister and of his deep humility and sacrificial spirit. He 'had one ambition,' Robert Lapsley said, 'and that was to be of service in the neediest places in the world.'[46]

After her husband's death Lucy Sheppard continued to serve at Grace Presbyterian Church in Louisville and spoke in other churches, both white and black, about foreign and home mission work. The Kentucky Synodical Woman's Auxiliary conferred on her a life membership in the organization. 'A lovely honour,' said Mrs Sheppard. Besides her ministry in the church and synod, she worked for the United States government as a case worker in 'social hygiene' for two years, and for the Family Service Organization of Louisville in a similar work for several more years. She visited needy homes, supplying food and clothes, friendship, and advice. 'Many cases of dire need and distress demanded all of my Christian faith and fortitude,' she wrote. When asked to sum up her life, Lucy Sheppard said simply, 'It is glorious to have lived and laboured for God.'[47] In 1940, shortly after writing those words, Lucy Gantt Sheppard died. Julia Lake Kellersberger concludes her booklet on *Lucy Gantt Sheppard: Shepherdess of His Sheep on Two Continents* with these words:

> Mrs Sheppard was a missionary of 'beginnings.' She began the first school in the American Presbyterian Congo Mission at Ibanche; she was instrumental in having printed the first book, a Hymnal, in the Tshiluba dialect; she witnessed the first baptismal service of the mission's converts among the Bakuba in 1895; she was present to welcome at Luebo the first arrival of the first mission steamer, the Lapsley; she was the first through-passenger on the first Congo railway; she was the first foreign woman to enter the Bakuba Kingdom; and she was the founder of the first Woman's Society of the Congo mission! She was a pioneer traveller; a pioneer homemaker; a pioneer linguist; a pioneer educator; and a pioneer missionary ... When she returned to America she pioneered among the women

of her own race in the South and aided them in more abundant living. Truly she deserves to be among the first in the hearts of her countrywomen—the shepherdess of His sheep on two continents![48]

On William Henry Sheppard's memorial stone in Louisville Cemetery are the simple words, 'He Lived for Others.' Those words are equally true of Lucy Gantt Sheppard, who was buried next to him. They brought the Bible's good news to the Congo and to their people in America.

*How beautiful are the feet of those
who preach the good news!*

8

JAMES A. BRYAN
(1863–1941)

He went about doing good.

JAMES BRYAN walked the streets of Birmingham, Alabama, ministering in the name of Jesus to the people of the fast-growing city—not only to respectable people but also, and especially, to gamblers, drunkards, and prostitutes.[1] Fast-growing Birmingham, named after the great industrial city of England, had hundreds of manufacturing plants and nearby mining companies. Bryan said that, unlike the businessmen who were moving to Birmingham to make money, he had nothing to invest 'but his life and his love.'[2] All the people of the city, black and white, native-born and immigrants, poor and rich, were his brothers and sisters. People loved him. He was, they said, 'the minister of the sympathetic heart.'[3] They called him 'Brother Bryan.'

James Alexander Bryan was born near Kingstree, South Carolina, on March 20, 1863, two years after South Carolina seceded from the Union. His parents were poor in money, but rich in faith. Every morning and evening the family gathered to sing a psalm or hymn, to read a passage from the Bible, and to kneel in prayer. At a little country school James studied reading, writing, arithmetic—and the Shorter Catechism. The Bryans were faithful members of the town's Presbyterian church. Hampden DuBose, a student at Columbia Theological Seminary, supplied the pulpit of their church during a summer vacation, and made a deep impression on young James. DuBose became a missionary to China, where he preached, planted churches, and fought the opium trade. He wrote the biography of the Southern Presbyterian missionary leader John Leighton Wilson.

James Bryan was sent by his parents to a prep school in North Carolina. He went on to the University of North Carolina, where he was known for his ability as a public speaker. After four years at the university, 'amid trials, temptations, triumphs, and lack of money,' he went north to Princeton Theological Seminary to prepare for the ministry, arriving in September 1886 with $1.85 in his pocket.[4] The piety of the slim young Southerner earned him the nickname 'the saint,' spoken not in mockery but seriously by his fellow students. Bryan loved his professors—William Henry Green, Alexander McGill, Caspar Wistar Hodge, and B. B. Warfield—and loved his studies, especially Bible and preaching. In Princeton Bryan worked at the Negro church on Witherspoon Street, teaching Sunday school and often leading the Wednesday prayer meeting. Here among black people he felt at home. Years later when his Princeton Seminary class gathered for its fortieth reunion, Bryan slipped away from the festivities, went to Witherspoon

Street Presbyterian Church, and preached to the people there.

A friend in Charleston, South Carolina, sent James Bryan a copy of *The Life of Trust* by George Müeller. Born in Germany, Müeller moved to Bristol, England, where he devoted his life to the care of orphan children, relying on voluntary contributions that flowed in through his prayers and the deep impression made by his life of trust in God. Bryan read *The Life of Trust* and was deeply moved. One day in Alexander Hall at the seminary, he quietly fell on his knees and rededicated his life to Christ, promising that from now on he would trust Him for everything, including direction in finding his life's work.

During the summer of 1888 Bryan served Third Presbyterian, a recently organized church in Birmingham, Alabama.[5] The next year he turned down a call to become assistant at a large church in Philadelphia to return to the church in Birmingham. It met in a small wooden building, with a congregation of thirty-seven members. Bryan's first sermon was from Luke 19:10—'For the Son of man is come to seek and to save that which was lost.' That became his message for the city. His biographer wrote, 'At the heart of all his preaching is his faith in the salvation provided for sinful men in Jesus Christ.'[6]

In 1890 James Bryan married Leonora Clayton Howze of Marion, Alabama. The Reverend Neal Anderson, a Princeton Seminary friend who was pastor of the Presbyterian church in Marion, assisted in the wedding. Leonora entered wholeheartedly into her husband's ministry. Years later Bryan said, 'All things come through prayer and absolute faith, but whatever I may be is due largely to the faithfulness of my wife. She has prayed for me and borne with me in my weakness, impatience, and lack of wisdom for years.'[7] The Bryan's first child, a little girl named Kekomoisa, meaning 'dear little one,' lived only a year. They had six more children, five boys and a girl. Bryan tried to spend time with his children, but his days and even his nights were busy. One night, his daughter, Mary, said, 'Father, why can't you stay with us here on the porch until bedtime?' The answer was 'Mary, I would love to stay with you, but I have to go now for Jesus' sake.'[8] As the children grew older he had them help him and they felt that they had a part in their father's 'work for God.'[9] The Bryans' six children embraced their parents' faith. Two sons became ministers. One of them served as a missionary in Japan until the tensions leading to war forced his return to the United States.

Money was always short in the Bryan household. When in need, the family prayed, 'Lord, send us a wedding.' In 1926 a reporter for the *Birmingham Post* estimated that during Bryan's thirty-seven years in the city he had married almost five thousand couples! Most of the money Brother Bryan received for conducting weddings, however, went into his ministry of mercy. The Bryans lived in a small cottage next-door to the church. In 1901, both the church and the cottage were destroyed by fire, caused by the exhaust of one of the great factories nearby. Everything was lost—books, sermons, clothes, furniture. Standing in the ruins, Bryan said, 'It is all right. The Lord is good.'[10] Bryan and his congregation set out to build a new church in a different location, surrounded by a community of hard-working men and women. There was only one way to build the church without going into debt—by prayer and hard work. Some years later Andrew Carnegie gave half the funds required for an organ.

Bryan's office at the church, it was said, contained just two books—a Bible and a telephone directory, both showing evidence of much use. From the Bible came the messages he preached. From the phone book came the names and phone numbers of people in Birmingham he knew or wanted to know. Brother Bryan preached to fifty or more 'congregations' each week, varying in size from five or six firemen seated around their fire truck to the one hundred and fifty people who came to his church. Before church services he went out and invited people on the street to come in, and when the church was full he began the service.

James Bryan preached at least six times a week. In his later years, he regularly preached on the radio—a new invention that he thought at first was 'of the devil' but soon called 'the Lord's own gift.'[11] Birmingham's main radio station gave him free time, a service it provided only to the American Legion and Brother Bryan. A radio announcer introduced him with the words, 'The best friend of Birmingham, Brother Bryan, will now speak.'[12] His messages were fifteen-minute Bible studies, simple, clear, and down to earth. Someone asked about Brother Bryan's radio broadcasts, 'What does he talk about?' 'Why, anything and everything,' came the reply, 'but always about Jesus Christ.'[13] For example, in a sermon from 2 Peter 1:19 ('Keep in mind the words of the prophets'), Bryan said that the prophet Isaiah, 'looked down through the centuries and saw Jesus.'[14] Bryan encouraged his listeners to look back to the Bible and up to heaven and see Jesus.

Bryan's office—it was called by his church members and friends 'the confessional'—saw a constant stream of visitors bringing their problems to the pastor. During the financial crash of 1929, some people were tempted to give up the struggle. One day the Birmingham newspaper carried a little notice that read: 'If you are discouraged, can't see a way out, and are thinking of ending it all, before you do anything come see me in the study at Twenty-second Street and Avenue G. Signed, J. A. Bryan.'[15] Within a month more than twenty-five people who were struggling with thoughts of suicide came to the pastor for help.

Brother Bryan was out in the city every day, visiting church members and others, helping those in need, witnessing to people, and praying with them. Calls came to larger, more prosperous churches, but, as Bryan wrote about one such call, 'I went to bed and had a vision of the hungry, starving, sick, blind, and helpless—that vision settled my life in Birmingham.'[16] God had sent him to Birmingham, Bryan believed, 'that the gospel might be preached to the poor.'[17] Jesus left us a legacy, he said, 'Ye have the poor with you always.' Bryan believed 'that the Gospel was best given to the hungry along with bread, that salvation was more likely to be effective for the naked along with clothing, that Christ was best preached to the homeless when one provided a place for them to lay their heads.'[18] Bryan wrote:

> Christ taught us to pray, 'Give us this day our daily bread.' If he gives you your daily bread, you should divide it with someone else ... People do not read

their Bibles, they read you and me ... Beneath that torn coat or ragged shawl, the life may be torn, but there is a soul for whom Jesus died and if we can but point that soul to Christ by our unselfish life, by our loving life, then we will do our part in leading the world to Christ.[19]

For years Brother Bryan conducted relief work with the poor throughout Birmingham, with a few helpers, but without bookkeeping, reports, or organization. When people sought to discover just how much he did, he was likely to reply, 'I don't know. I am too busy to keep records. We leave that to the angels.'[20] How did he do it all? Bryan replied, 'We do not carry it on, but God does.'[21] It is his 'own work.'[22] Food and money were brought to Brother Bryan every day. On the first of each month an envelope containing twenty-five new one-dollar bills mysteriously appeared on his desk, or was slipped under his door, with a note, 'For God's poor and hungry.'[23] Brother Bryan was always deeply moved by the needs of people he met in the city. More than once he came home at night without his overcoat, having given it away to someone he thought needed it more than he did. Some members of Third Presbyterian and other downtown churches wandered off to wealthier congregations in the suburbs. Since there was need, suffering, and sin all around them in the city, Bryan saw no reason to move his church to 'a more desirable location.' He wanted to stay in the heart of the city.

Brother Bryan sometimes gave lectures at Columbia Theological Seminary in Atlanta on pastoral theology. He told the students: 'The pastor must live on his knees.'[24]

'When you pay a pastoral visit talk very little about yourself and a great deal about Jesus.'[25] 'Love people into the kingdom of God's love.'[26] 'Ever since I have been a pastor, my work has been partially among needy people. If there are no poor in your congregation, my humble advice is to get another charge or shut up your doors.'[27]

Bryan got to know a young Scot, Peter Marshall, who had come to Birmingham to work for the newspaper. Marshall, who taught the Men's Bible Class in a local church, decided to go to Columbia Seminary and study for the ministry. When he was ready to go he found that he did not have the six-dollar train fare to Atlanta. In *A Man Called Peter*, the biography of her husband, Catherine Marshall explained what happened. 'Peter was invited to drive to Decatur with the Reverend James A. Bryan, who was to deliver the opening lectures at the seminary. This friend, Birmingham's beloved "Brother Bryan," was to have a profound influence on Peter's life and ministry.'[28] Peter Marshall became a famous preacher at New York Avenue Presbyterian Church in Washington, D. C., and chaplain of the United States Senate.

To help their pastor in his work, the children of Brother Bryan's church raised money to buy him a little pony, which they named 'Cheerful Endeavor.' Later Bryan was given a horse and buggy by a group of men; they had raised some of the money they needed in a poker game! Bryan called the magnificent dappled gray horse 'Robert,' and then added a second name, 'Extension.' 'Robert Extension' expanded Bryan's ministry throughout the city, as did an automobile given to him in later years. Brother Bryan was a notoriously bad driver, his attention usually on other things besides the road and traffic signs. Bryan said that he preferred his pony and his horse who knew where to go without much direction. Brother Bryan was welcomed into the homes, factories, hospitals, schools, and jails of Birmingham. The restaurants of the city never charged him or anyone who came with him. Many of the people of Birmingham worked in the city's factories. They elected the pastor to honorary membership in their unions. He contributed his simple Bible sermons to their periodicals. The firemen and policemen of the city felt that Brother Bryan belonged especially to them. He selected the fire truck, Big Pump No. 1, to be the hearse at his funeral.

Brother Bryan lived in Birmingham during years of strict segregation and growing racial tension. He loved the African Americans who crowded into the city. Toward the end of his life he said, 'I wish to show my gratitude to the Negro race and to God, who put them at our door, by trying to do more for them as I near the end of the pilgrimage of life.' On Sunday mornings at five o'clock, Bryan met and prayed with his 'coloured friends.' 'They get up early to go to their work of preparing breakfast in the homes of others,' he said. 'I meet them on the street as I go to church and we stop and have prayer together.' In his biography of Bryan, Hunter Blakely wrote in 1934, 'Suppose Birmingham with its vast Negro population should have a race riot, is there any man who could step between the races and bring peace? Ask that question of any thoughtful man in the city and undoubtedly his reply would be, "Yes, there is one, Brother Bryan."'[29]

Brother Bryan was famous for his frequent prayers—short and to the point. Facing the squalor of the city and the struggles of its people, Bryan prayed over and over, 'O Lord, help us fight the devil.' When the state legislature passed a bill to submit to a referendum the question of opening theatres and other places of amusement on Sundays, some met to organize opposition to the move. Bryan was asked to open the meeting with prayer. He bowed silently for a moment and then prayed, 'O God, help us to live like Christ and fight like hell! Amen.'[30] He prayed with new immigrants who could not understand what he said but appreciated what he did. Brother Bryan was the only man, it was said, who could walk into any poolroom in the city and quietly say 'Let us pray,' and every cap would come off and every head would bow.[31] Bryan's telephone probably carried 'more prayers each day than any telephone in all the world.'[32] Bryan would call scores of people and say, 'I just called you to have a little prayer.'[33]

A Birmingham newspaper reported that during rush hour, a young woman in a great hurry came down the sidewalk but was stopped when the light at the corner turned red. 'Oh, damn,' she said. A hand touched her arm gently, and she heard a quiet voice, saying, 'Sister, let us pray. O Lord, give us both patience to bear with these traffic lights. Amen.'[34] One day Brother Bryan was robbed by a man with a gun. He took the minister's watch and the small amount of money he had. He was astonished to hear Bryan say, 'Brother, let us pray.' When Bryan finished his prayer the man returned the watch and money and fled![35] One day Brother Bryan approached a policeman directing traffic.

'Are you a Christian, brother?' he asked. Without taking his eyes off the cars, the policeman said, 'No.' Then Bryan prayed that the man might come to Christ—and he did!

In 1920 the *Birmingham News* announced that the paper would present a 'Loving Cup' worth $500 to the person who had given the greatest service to the city during that year. A committee appointed to make the choice considered fifty-three people for the first award and decided unanimously on Brother Bryan. For the presentation ceremony one of the largest theatres in Birmingham was filled, with hundreds turned away. Religious leaders of the city gave speeches, including Dr Morris Newfield, the rabbi of Temple Emanuel. The rabbi and the minister were devoted friends and frequently sat down together with their Hebrew Bibles to translate for themselves and discuss some Old Testament passage. Dr Newfield said: 'I have known Dr Bryan longer perhaps than any of the speakers. I knew him here twenty-five years ago and he has not changed. He is still the same Brother Bryan … He is the most beloved man in our city … I have never seen a man who caught the message of Jesus and illustrated it so tenderly and gently and splendidly as Brother Bryan, for, deeply spiritual, he has caught that message and, following Jesus, is going about doing good … He is the noblest, sweetest spirit I have ever known.'[36] Labour leaders paid tribute to Bryan; one called him 'a labourer's brother.' 'All working men know Brother Bryan,' he said. 'He labours with them and they will work their hands off for him.' In accepting the Loving Cup, Brother Bryan quoted David Livingstone, who wrote in his diary, 'Jesus, my Lord, my King, My God, I again rededicate my life and my service to Thee, and to the furtherance of Thy kingdom.'[37] The next year Brother Bryan was expected to give the opening prayer at the ceremony honouring the winner of the 'Loving Cup' for 1921. He phoned to say that he could not be there for the opening prayer—he had an important funeral that afternoon—but he thought it would be possible for him to offer a prayer at the end of the meeting. The funeral was for a 'redeemed harlot' whom he had led 'in her last illness to the Saviour.' He had promised her that he would conduct her funeral, and he did.[38] And he made it in time for the last prayer for the 'Loving Cup' ceremony.

Worn out by his labours, Bryan became seriously ill in 1922. He was sent to a hospital in Mobile, Alabama, to recover. After three months in the hospital and a time of further rest in the North Carolina mountains, Bryan returned to his beloved Birmingham. The News happily reported:

> Brother Bryan is coming back. That was the big news of Tuesday … Pretty soon, God willing, he will be the same old earnest, loving, compassionate Bryan passing through the byways and hedges of Greater Birmingham looking for the helpless and the afflicted, the scorned, the broken, blessing them, giving the cup of water, the loaf of bread, and whatever money he may have in his purse.[39]

After five more years without a vacation, Bryan experienced another physical breakdown. Mrs Bryan decided that the only way to get her husband away from the city was with a trip to the Holy Land. She knew that 'if anything could draw him away from Birmingham, it would be the country of his Bible.'[40] She consulted with a few of his friends and they agreed. A citywide effort raised the $4,000 for the trip for Bryan and his wife. Mrs Bryan's health prevented her going, but Harry Bryan, their youngest son, who was a student at Columbia Seminary, accompanied his father. At their departure a huge crowd filled the train station. The police band played hymns and patriotic songs, and Brother Bryan led them all in praying together the Lord's Prayer.

Bryan and his son first visited Scotland. Bryan was delighted with Blantyre, the town of David Livingstone. Here the humble village workmen reminded him of his own hard-working poor in Birmingham and he stopped them on the streets, as if he were at home, to have prayer with them. Bryan enjoyed Edinburgh with its Presbyterian history. In England father and son went to Cambridge and Oxford, then on to the Netherlands, France, and Switzerland. Geneva held Bryan's attention because it was the city of John Calvin. He thought that it was 'one of the best places we have seen so far.' In Rome they visited the Mamertine Prison, the catacombs, and the Appian Way, 'which thrilled his soul.' They sailed from Naples to Athens, where they visited Mars Hill 'for Paul's sake' and drove out 'to a refugee camp to find the mother of a Birmingham restaurant friend.'[41] They went to Constantinople, and then at last reached their goal—the Holy Land. In the tour bus Brother Bryan was given a front seat, where he sat with his open Bible, rejoicing in the biblical sites and regretting his inability to witness to the people and pray with them in their language.

Bryan was rested, delighted with what he had seen and experienced, and eager to get home. The morning newspaper announced that Brother Bryan would arrive in Birmingham on a certain afternoon at three o'clock. When his train pulled into the station, hundreds of people were there, as were the police and the firemen's bands. When Brother Bryan and Harry appeared, the crowd rushed forward to greet them, and, in that way they knew so well, he lifted his hands and said, 'Let us pray.'[42]

In 1930, on his sixty-seventh birthday, the City Commission of Birmingham appointed Bryan the official chaplain of the city. A reporter of the *Birmingham Post* asked Bryan to write for the Saturday paper about what Christ had done for him during his life. He wrote:

> Words cannot express what Christ has meant and does mean to me. Books can never tell it. Songs can never tell it. Artists can never put it on canvas. He has been the all to the writer. In sorrow He has been my comfort. In trouble He has been my stay. In need He has been my supply. In darkness He has been my light. In the rough places He has been my guide.
>
> When I have almost despaired and fallen, He has kept me from falling. He has preserved my going out and my coming in. We think of Him, and rightly so, as our Saviour from sin and all its direful consequences. So said the angel in the annunciation: 'His name shall be called Jesus for he shall save His people from their sins.' We think of Him as our Redeemer, because in Him we have redemption from sin through His shed blood, His atoning blood. His blood is the ground of our redemption, and faith is the means.

Christ has been the sufficient Christ to me in temptations. He knows the feelings of our infirmities, the weakness of humanity, because He lived on earth in flesh and was tempted as we are. And so He says, 'My grace is sufficient for thee, my strength is made perfect in thy weakness.' Christ to me has been my Mediator. It is truly wonderful to think of the fact that if we sin we have an advocate, a mediator, even Jesus Christ the righteous. It is wonderful to think that He pleads for us poor, failing, falling, believing sinners.

He has been my helper. Many times when I did not know where to turn, I would think of Him and He would say, 'I will strengthen thee, yea, I will uphold thee with the right hand of my righteousness.' Many times when I was a student at Princeton, I was without means and money, and tried in many ways, discouraged, but Christ never failed to help me. Many times in a pastorate of nearly forty-one years, where trials have met at every turn of the way and discouragements assailed me, Christ has always helped me. He has never deserted me to my foes.

He has sustained me through temptations, trials, sorrows, really through all the tragedies and blood and tears of this world, and increased my faith and hope of eternal life. To me He has been the author and finisher of my faith, who for the joy that was set before Him endured the cross. This has made me endlessly patient, more heroic in His cause, and above all happy in Him.

My heart overflows when *i* write this humbly, with a small dot over a small i, that it was Christ who did it, for Christ has meant everything to this church and to this pastor.[43]

On July 29, 1934, a statue of Brother Bryan kneeling in prayer was dedicated in a service at the Highlands Methodist Church. The church was filled to the doors, but the man they had come to honour was not to be seen. He had slipped in quietly and was sitting at the back of the church, where an usher spotted him and led him to the front. Senator Hugo L. Black, later justice of the United States Supreme Court, was the speaker. 'Let us hope,' he said, that this statue 'will inspire those here today, and those who also know Brother Bryan, to love our neighbour as ourselves.'[44] The statue, made of Alabama white marble, became one of Birmingham's landmarks.[45]

Ernie Pyle, famous war correspondent and journalist, visited Bryan when Bryan was seventy-three years old. He wrote in January 1936 an article for the *Washington Daily News* under the caption, 'Portrait of a Good Samaritan: Brother Bryan of Birmingham.' Pyle wrote, 'As soon as you land in Birmingham you hear of Brother Bryan. Everyone knows him. He is a tradition … They think of him as the one man who lives as the best of us profess to live, but don't … Despite his age, Brother Bryan's activities right now would make a football player look like an invalid.'[46]

On June 28, 1939, Brother Bryan's golden anniversary of ministry in Birmingham was celebrated in the Municipal Auditorium. All races and people from every walk of life were represented on the stage and in the audience of more than four thousand people. Often during his long ministry in Birmingham, Bryan had said, 'I loved this city from the first and still love it.'[47] Bryan's last days of ministry were from his sickbed, as he directed his work of evangelism and mercy. The Brother Bryan Mission was founded in 1940, shortly before Bryan died, to fulfil his last wish for a shelter where homeless men could find 'a meal, a bed, and God's love.' Bryan's last sermon in the *Birmingham Post* was about 'God's Love.'[48]

Leonora Bryan died on March 4, 1940. The Bryans had been married for forty-nine years. Brother Bryan died less than a year later, on January 28, 1941. During his last minutes on earth, his son James heard him say, 'So many people.' Thinking that he meant there were too many people in the room, he asked his father if he wanted them to leave. 'So many people,' he answered, 'without Christ.'[49] The whole city was in sorrow. Two hours before the funeral service Third Presbyterian Church was packed. Thousands gathered outside to listen over the public-address system. 'In that throng were all kinds of people—saints and sinners, rich and poor, folks in fine raiment and others in patched clothing. Jews, Greek Orthodox and Roman Catholics and Protestants were there.'[50] At three o'clock the flag over City Hall was lowered to half-mast. Stores closed in downtown Birmingham, and the simple service began. By a long-standing agreement with his friends at the fire station, Brother Bryan's body was carried to the cemetery in the big red fire truck.

Brother Bryan was loved, remembered, and honoured because, like his Master, 'he went about doing good' (Acts 10:38). He walked the streets of Birmingham, in the day and at night, in the heat of summer and the cold of winter, finding those he could help and telling them the good news about Jesus. On June 7, 1914, the *Birmingham Age Herald* ended an editorial about Brother Bryan with these words: 'We who have watched his footsteps see the tracks which he has left among the desolate and distressed.'[51]

> *How beautiful are the feet of those*
> *who preach the good news!*

9

BOB CHILDRESS
(1890–1956)

The man who moved a mountain.

THE Blue Ridge Mountains of southern Virginia are blessed with lovely peaks and valleys—and, a hundred years ago, with chestnut trees, a bounty so generous that people said that the chestnuts were like the manna sent by God to feed the children of Israel. But the mountains were also full of trouble. The people once were given to whiskey made in moonshine stills in hidden places, and to guns and violence. They feared outsiders, despised 'book learning,' and nursed grievances for generations. Their religion, such as it was, was shaped mostly by Hardshell Baptists, who taught that a stern and grim Deity controlled everything, and that it really did not matter very much what people did.

In Patrick County, on the eastern slope of Virginia's Blue Ridge, just above the North Carolina line, Bob Childress was born on January 19, 1890, while a blizzard howled across the mountains.[1] Bob's ancestors were Scotch-Irish who had been in these mountains for three generations. His parents and eight brothers and sisters lived in a one-room cabin. The girls slept on the dirt floor of the cabin and the boys in the loft. His mother and father were hard-working and hard-drinking people. 'We were the poorest in a place where everyone was poor,' Bob said.[2]

The Quakers started a school in The Hollow, where the Childress family lived, and Bob attended classes. But when the pretty young teacher left to get married, Bob didn't go to school at all except for a day or two now and then. When he was still a boy, Bob learned to 'fight mean,' to drink, and to gamble. His first memory was getting drunk when he was not quite three years old. At the age of eleven he saw the body of a man who had been hanged from the limb of a gumwood tree. When he was fifteen, he earned five dollars cutting timber, bought his first pair of long pants and a pistol, and at last 'felt like a man.'[3] Bob was already over six feet tall, 'lean and hard as a chestnut tree,' and was known as a 'heller.' He was hardly ever sober. Twice he went out in the woods and put his pistol to his temple, but did not pull the trigger. 'I can't tell you why,' he said.[4]

One day Bob wandered into a little Methodist church where a revival service was going on. When the altar call was given, he went forward and knelt at the rail. He went back to the church each night. 'That week of revival didn't change me into a new man,' Bob said, 'but it gave me the first real peace in my whole life. For the first time I felt a power stronger than the power of liquor and guns.'[5] Bob's brother Hasten, fourteen years older than Bob and more like a father to him, faced him with a choice. 'Bob, what you doin' with your life? You log a little, blacksmith a little, and a little this and that, but mostly drink and raise hell. Now I'll tell you. You're a learner. You got to go back to school. You're one Childress who can make somethin' of himself.'[6]

The next week Bob, twenty-one years old, entered the eighth grade at the Quaker school. He at once fell in love with fellow student Pearl Ayers, a timid, brown-eyed slip of a girl he had known all his life, and decided to marry her. One day he piled her things in a wagon and took her to a Methodist parsonage down in the valley. The marriage ceremony was over before anyone could stop it. Bob and Pearl were happy together, but it was the end of his schooling—and hers too. Bob gave up drinking. On Sundays he rented a horse and buggy and drove with Pearl from one church service to another. They had a baby boy, Conduff, and a little girl, Evelyn. When a flu epidemic swept through The Hollow, Pearl died, and Bob was devastated. He thought of drink. He thought of suicide. One night he found himself repeating the Lord's Prayer. 'Our Father,' he began dispiritedly, then stopped at the line 'Thy will be done.' 'Not my own will,' he said, 'which till now had somehow always been served, but *thy* will, God's will.' Perhaps in this awful moment, he thought, God had another plan, one so distant there was no hint of it. When his own will could do nothing, maybe he should let God do the planning. Peace surged over him as it had on that strange night at the revival.[7]

Bob rented a house, put up a blacksmith shop just behind it, and opened a grocery store in one room of the house. This way he was able to work all day and into the night at home and care for his little children at the same time. A young preacher, Roy Smith, fresh out of seminary, came to The Hollow.[8] Roy was starting Sunday schools, and asked Bob to help him. Roy did not tell Bob that he was a Presbyterian, because anyone who sprinkled babies and called it baptism was considered an infidel by the Hardshell Baptists of the mountains. Angered at the continuing violence and drunkenness around him, Bob had himself sworn in as a deputy sheriff. Two years as a deputy, however, were enough to convince him that the law would never control the proud people of the Blue Ridge. He turned in his badge and opened his smithy again.

Bob married Lelia Montgomery, who was known as the prettiest girl in The Hollow. She was crippled, but she had the gift of serenity. Bob and his children loved her. On Sundays the family would make their way by horse and buggy to some 'brush arbor' Sunday school, where Bob taught the rough mountain children. He threatened the unruly and often-drunken boys by saying, 'If I can't teach the love of God into you, I'll beat the devil out of you!' They knew he meant it. He continued his blacksmith business to support his family, taught the lower grades in the local school, and began to preach, going some Sundays to nearby Squirrel Creek, where the African Americans who lived there had a little chapel. People began to notice what Bob was doing and several churches tried to recruit him for their work. Bob told them, 'I'm too dry for the Baptists, don't have enough religion for Methodists, and am too ignorant for the Presbyterians.'[9]

When Bob learned that Roy Smith was a Presbyterian, he and Lelia and the children were baptized in the

Presbyterian church. Bob began in earnest to prepare for the ministry. He borrowed books from Smith and studied deep into the night. He read the Gospels over and over. He began to better understand what God was like by seeing what Jesus was like. One day a man from Buffalo Mountain, eight miles north of The Hollow, stopped to have Bob repair his horse's loose shoe. While Bob worked, the man told tales of life on the Buffalo—'a right wild place' of lonely women and frightened children and twisted ways that led people to kill and enjoy talking about it. Bob decided he wanted to help people like that. He wanted to be a preacher in the worst places in the mountains.

Bob Childress was a man of thirty with a wife and four children. Lelia said, 'Bob, if it's a Presbyterian preacher you must be, we have no time to lose.'[10] He studied nights with the same fervour with which he pounded out ploughshares. He bought a big black mule, and on the opening day of school at the Friends Mission, six miles away, he mounted the mule and set off to begin high school. Behind him, clutching his pants pockets, was little Conduff, who was starting first grade. Lelia stood in the doorway and waved. To Bob it seemed like a silent benediction.

Bob was soon promoted to the tenth grade. By spring he had learned all he could in the mountain school and decided to go on to college—Davidson College, Roy Smith's alma mater. In September the Childress family moved to Davidson, North Carolina, two hundred miles away. Bob spent the next summer as student pastor in a place not far above his home in a community known as Mayberry, halfway between The Hollow and Buffalo Mountain. He walked from place to place to preach, carrying a portable pulpit on his shoulder. Loud and stormy in the pulpit, Bob was gentle outside it, caring for the many lonely, overlooked people who struggled with danger and poverty in their beautiful Blue Ridge mountains.

Bob decided that he couldn't take more time for college. He wanted to start seminary at once. One day he and Roy Smith set off for Richmond, where Union Theological Seminary trained Southern Presbyterian pastors. The registrar was startled when Bob asked to be admitted—a man who had had only one year of high school and one year of college, with a wife and five children, and no money! The seminary president, Dr Walter W. Moore, said, 'We'd like to help, Mr Childress, but our responsibility is turning out qualified ministers. We can't relax our standards. Maybe you'd better give up the idea of the ministry. There are other ways of serving.'[11]

Bob talked the seminary into letting him attend classes without being enrolled. He was older than the other students, unpolished in his mountain ways, and ignorant of many things, but he was determined to become a Presbyterian minister. After his last class each day he hurried home to help Lelia with the children, and then studied late into the night. The man from The Hollow began to impress his teachers and fellow students. The *Presbyterian Survey* wrote about Bob Childress:

> When he entered Union Seminary no one thought he could do the work. He was refused a scholarship or a house rent free as would normally have been his due as a married student. Nevertheless, in the first semester he made a high record in every class. Dr Walter W.

Moore, who at first had advised him against the ministry, came to him and personally apologized. Instead of giving him one scholarship, Dr Moore gave him two, and his choice of all the houses on the campus. The First Presbyterian Church of Richmond, to their eternal credit, gave several hundred dollars a year to keep him in the seminary.[12]

During his studies Bob continued to serve the church at Mayberry in the mountains, driving to Mayberry twice a month, and spending his summers there. Bob's people at Mayberry built their own church, one of the earliest Presbyterian buildings in all the Blue Ridge. Bob studied preaching in seminary but learned better how to preach from the people in the mountains. One day he was explaining a theological lesson that he had had in seminary to Abe Webb: 'Moses gave us the laws, Abe. Jesus gave us love. Without love there can be no forgiveness. Where law strikes, love heals. Law and love walk side by side.' Abe's wife, Lila, was listening. 'Why don't you say that tomorrow in church?' she asked. 'Just the way you said it now. We'll understand.'[13] Bob discovered that he did not have to shout to make people hear, but to be simple and clear, and to use humour in his preaching, which he learned was a healing balm.

During his last year in seminary Bob Childress was invited to preach in prominent Richmond churches and several times at Central Presbyterian in Washington, Woodrow Wilson's church. Wilson was born at Staunton in the Shenandoah Valley, a little more than a hundred miles along the Blue Ridge from The Hollow. Bob could not get over it, a mountain boy from The Hollow preaching in the church of the president of the United States!

The day Bob graduated from Union Seminary, a church in North Carolina sent an elder to offer him a call, promising a fine manse, a new car, and a salary beyond anything he could have imagined. He was thrilled. He had some debts to pay and the care of a wife and seven children. He promised to give his answer in the morning. Late that night a stranger stopped at Bob's desk in the seminary library, introduced himself as Dr Clark, a member of Montgomery Presbytery, and said, 'We've got a field in the mountains where they're shooting each other, they're ignorant, they don't have a chance, they have no schools or Sunday schools. There's enough work there to kill you, but we'll furnish you a living while you're at it.' The mission field was Buffalo Mountain, almost four thousand feet high and no more than ten miles from The Hollow, with Mayberry between. The summit of the mountain looked like a charging buffalo, head lowered, hump bulging, a thousand feet above the surrounding hills. It had the reputation as the most lawless region in all the Southern mountains. 'I'm a mountain man, Dr Clark,' Bob said. 'I believe that's where the Lord wants me to go.'

But it was not where Lelia wanted to go. She told her husband, 'I can't help what I feel, Bob, and I'm plain frightened. No amount of talkin' is goin' to make me want to go. But talk isn't goin' to change you either. You're set on it. So we'll go, and I'll try, and we'll hope you are right.'[14] Lelia came to love Buffalo Mountain as much or more than Bob did. She said to him, 'I guess you or the Lord, or both of you must have been right.'[15] After Bob died Lelia continued to live near the church on Buffalo Mountain.

Thirty-six years old, his life already half spent, Bob Childress was taking on Buffalo Mountain. The Childress family were the first outsiders to move there in a hundred years. There were those who said that Bob Childress would not last the summer. Bob prayed that God would show him the way and give him the strength to shake the Buffalo to its granite core. It was not easy to be a preacher and pastor in such a hard place of hates and fears, but Bob did not give up, or even slow down. 'Murmuring will not take the place of marching,' he said.[16] People said that Bob worked like a man either running from the devil, or after him! Bob had an engaging sense of humour that he used to good advantage in the pulpit and out of it. One day he picked up an old mountaineer and said, 'Come along with me to church.' 'Nope,' said the man, then after a pause, 'too many hypocrites.' 'Aw, come on,' said Bob laughing. 'There's always room for one more!'[17]

The Hardshell Baptists feared the inroads that Bob was making on the mountain—starting schools and Sunday schools, and holding night services, all of which they bitterly opposed. They despised his education and mocked his baptismal practice of sprinkling. One man said that Bob did not baptize, he dry-cleaned. He did not believe in their kind of predestination and he didn't drink. One said to him, 'Man, don't you believe that what will be, will be?' 'Well,' was Bob's answer, 'I don't believe what won't be, will be.'[18] With his openness and kindness he befriended the Hardshells, completely winning over their most prominent preacher in the lower Blue Ridge.

Bob started the Buffalo Mountain Mission School but soon found, he said, that education wasn't the greatest need the people had. They needed a Saviour. He preached to them the gospel of God's redeeming love. Many came to

Bob's services, but few joined his church. Mountain people took their vows seriously. They were not about to give up their old ways and serve the Lord unless they meant it. 'Just come to the Lord, and let the Lord cure your soul first,' Bob told them. 'Then you can start to work on your drinking.'[19]

Used to the loud harangues of the Hardshell preachers, some found Bob's sermons disappointing. 'Oh, he talks good enough,' said one mountaineer, but you can't call it preaching.' Bob preached earnest, short, simple sermons with application to the people's lives and needs. Preaching on Job, he said:

> Job's first tests were years of property, power, family, the love of friends. His faith didn't depend on home or health or worldly applause. The secret—the ability to see and the willingness to look for God's hands in everything. Do you see God's hands in the full corn-crib, the full smokehouse, strong bodies? And do you still look for his hand in the storm or in the sickbed, or when you lose something, or by an open grave or the side of a suffering friend, or in the hard breathing or the hot brow of a little child? If you are enjoying life's blessings, the hand of God is there. If you are feeling life's losses, his hand is still there.[20]

The year 1929 was hard for the nation because of the Great Depression, and in the mountains a blight killed the chestnut trees. But on Buffalo Mountain there was a new church building, the last stone of which had been put in place the week of the stock market crash. On a trip to Tennessee to tell about his mission, Bob had seen churches built with fieldstone, and he sided the Buffalo Mountain Church in the same way. When Bob suggested that they use the native white stone for the church, one old mountaineer objected, saying, 'I have cussed every rock in the county trying to make a stalk of corn grow, and I can't stand to see rock in a church wall!'[21] Most people, however, thought it was a good plan, and it made an attractive church building.[22]

A new outbreak of violence shook the Buffalo community and shocked the pastor. Bob went to the church alone and prayed, 'O Lord, how long wilt thou be angry against the prayer of my people? Thou feedest them with the bread of tears, and givest them tears to drink in great measure.' After four years of hard work, Bob feared that Buffalo Mountain was more troubled than when he had come. He remembered a remark made by a missionary who spoke to the students at the seminary: 'The man who civilizes the Blue Ridge will be one who lives among the mountaineers, and whose family will set a pattern for Christian love and decency every day of the week.' That is what Bob Childress and his family did. There were encouraging signs that by God's grace the Christian message was getting through to hard and stubborn hearts. One night a man stopped the preacher after a prayer meeting. 'Bob,' he said, 'I ain't a-goin' home till I accept Christ as my Saviour.'[23]

The roads improved, owing largely to Bob's determination to make them better. He called them 'avenues of mercy.' With better roads he could serve more congregations. By 1938 he was travelling to eight churches, preaching and holding Sunday school at least once a week at each place. He was preaching to more than seven hundred people. There were a thousand or so children in his Sunday schools. Bob Childress spent much time taking people to the hospital or to the doctor, signing loans to help them buy a house or a farm, reaching out to the down-and-outs, paying fines for people in jail, some of whom were there because of charges he had brought against them for disturbing church services. On one occasion Bob and some of the men of the church caught fifteen young men throwing rocks at the church building, breaking the windows, and hauled them off to court. When the justice was about to sentence them, Bob interceded. 'They're good boys, judge,' he said. They just don't behave.' Bob's brother Hasten said, 'Bob always seems to think with his feelings instead of his head.' Bob bought and set up a sawmill that was soon giving people work and money. A fellow minister said of Bob Childress, 'He rewrote the first commandment of the mountains. It's no longer "My family is my care and keep." Now it's "Whoever's in need is my care and keep."'[24]

Many people had come to love the genial, generous preacher, but there were others who hated him. Not infrequently he found himself facing an angry moonshiner or someone who despised him for some other reason. One night Bob was driving home from a late church service when four men flagged him down as if they wanted a ride. The moment he stopped they pulled him out of the car. 'What is it you want of me?' he asked. 'We're just a-goin' to kill you, is all,' said one. When he saw that each was armed with a long knife, Bob was sure they meant it. He said calmly, 'If you're going to kill me that ought to be easy, for there are four of you. But let me have a prayer before I die.' He went to his knees and prayed out loud for the men and their eternal souls and for their families and for all the people of the mountains who had never learned to love. He concluded with the Lord's Prayer, asking the four men to join him. There was no sound from them until he finished, when he heard a single 'amen.' He got to his feet. No one moved. The men had sheathed their knives. He asked if they wanted a ride. They all climbed in.[25]

More and more people were being won to Christ—or at least to Bob Childress or to both. Bob had a way of speaking lovingly to people in need. He told one man who was burdened with his sin, 'The man who knows sin is the man who knows forgiveness.' 'Where was the Lord when our Muriel died?' a brokenhearted mother asked him. Bob said, 'Where was the Lord when his own Son was dying on the cross? Don't you think the Lord felt the same pain you feel?'[26] At the dismay and anger of some of the mountaineers, Bob befriended a group of gypsies who had come to nearby Slate Mountain, where Bob had started and built a church. He visited his black friends at Squirrel Creek and preached for them.

'Bringing people together is the one thing I've tried to do, but we haven't done enough yet,' Bob told his wife. 'And now's the time.' His white congregations, he believed, needed to meet the black Christians of Squirrel Creek and feel their warmth, their honesty and kindness. One Sunday he drove down to Squirrel Creek to preach in their chapel. After his sermon he asked the choir to sing for him. 'Now that sounds so much like the very heartbeat of heaven,' he said, 'that all Christians ought to hear it.' He invited the choir to sing at his Bluemont Church, just a few miles above on the ridge, though almost no one from Squirrel Creek had ever been there. A few weeks later Bob brought the black choir to a service at the Willis Church and took the whole group home for dinner. 'I never saw anyone so happy in my life as Mr Childress that day,' said the Squirrel Creek choir director. 'He kept going around with platters of fried chicken and boatloads of gravy, turnip greens, hot rolls, and mashed potatoes, then cake and peaches.'[27]

On Sundays Bob picked up some of the Squirrel Creek members and took them with him to visit his churches. When one woman said that she was fearful of going into a white church, Bob told her, 'Now, Sister Nora, my skin is light and yours is dark, but there's no difference in heaven. It's the colour of the soul that counts.' For more than a year Bob's churches held integrated meetings, and everybody—white and black—enjoyed them. But Bob wanted more. He wanted 'the brotherhood of black and white to be a deeper, working thing.'[28] Bob's last Sunday at his beloved Slate Mountain Church was Communion Sunday. He invited the folks from Squirrel Mountain to come and sing—and take Communion with the white congregation.

Bob suffered a stroke on a hot day in August 1950, while he was loading stones on a truck for an addition to one of his fourteen churches. Doctors told him he would have to give up preaching and rest more. But he could not stop. He continued to preach at four or five of his churches. When calls came from a hospital asking for the pastor, he was up and out no matter what the time or the weather.

One old man invited Bob to go for a walk with him on a summer's day when the flame azaleas were in full colour and the sun was shining. 'I've always been in debt,' the man said. 'But now I'm out. I don't owe nobody. Except you. I owe you. It's something I need to tell you, and it better be now.' He hesitated, searching for words. 'It's that you've tamed this here old Buffalo. You've given us all our "upright." You've made us see what fools we were with our drinking and fighting. And we never gave you anything back but ...' Bob stopped him, 'Yes, you did, more than you guess.'[29]

Just a week before Bob died, Hasten Childress sat in a rocker on his porch and talked about his brother. Bob used to say that each of us is tending the little patch of ground God lends us. 'Whatever comes to me in the pod,' he'd say, 'I want to pass on in full flower, and what comes to me in flower, I'd like to pass on in full fruit.' Well, the plants he tended are still bearing.[30] A growing number of Bob's young church members were called to Christian service elsewhere. 'Just imagine,' he thought to himself, 'old Buffalo Mountain a seedbed for missionaries.'[31]

Just before Christmas Bob Childress had a heart attack, and three weeks later, on January 16, 1956, he died at Roanoke Memorial Hospital. His grandson, Stewart Childress, who became pastor of three of the mountain churches that Bob began, said,

> Throughout the years many people have commented on what a great man Bob Childress was. They are impressed by the impact he had on people and say he won many souls for Christ. But my grandfather would be the first to say that he personally never won a single soul for Christ, it was the power of the Holy Spirit working through him. Without that power to sustain and guide him, he would not have had a fruitful ministry. The beauty of his story is that it demonstrates how

God uses ordinary people to accomplish extraordinary things.[32]

In his last years, Bob Childress made quick trips to cities in the Southeast, where he told about his ministry to mountain people. 'We go to the mountains,' he said, 'for their sake and for our own sake. And we go for Christ's sake. He loved them all, whether in the hills or the lowlands, whether white or black, scholar or simpleton, rich or poor. And in the last day our greatest joy will be to hear him say, "Inasmuch as you have been faithful unto one of the least of these, you have been faithful unto me."'[33] Bob Childress was faithful. By faith he moved a mountain.

> By faith this mountain shall be moved
> and the pow'r of the gospel shall prevail
> for we know in Christ all things are possible
> for all who call upon His name.[34]

How beautiful upon the [Appalachian] mountains are the feet of him who brings good news, who publishes peace, who brings good news of happiness, who publishes salvation, who says to Zion, 'Your God reigns!'
(Isaiah 52:7).

10

MARY BEAM
(1911–2002)
and
BETTY CRIDLAND
(1907–2003)

In the heart of the tall grass.

MARY BEAM AND BETTY CRIDLAND were loved by hundreds of American Christians, and their work in the 'heart of the tall grass' in the Sudan was followed eagerly and prayerfully.[1] The two missionaries were usually considered together and almost always called 'Mary and Betty'. My wife and I gave our little daughter, Isabel, a new doll one Christmas and she promptly named it 'Mary and Betty'!

Mary Sarah Beam was born in Greenville, South Carolina, on December 10, 1911. The fourth child of Mr and Mrs Clarence Beam, she grew up with older brothers, developing toughness and a love for sports. She entered Greenville Women's College (now Furman University), and to help pay her expenses, worked as a referee for the basketball games. Her Sunday school teacher persuaded her to spend at least one year at the new Columbia Bible College in Columbia, South Carolina. She stayed more than a year, and graduated in 1934.

Anna Elizabeth ('Betty') Cridland was born in Philadelphia, on July 8, 1907, the child of Edna Allen and John Laird Cridland. Her mother died at twenty-six years old, when Betty had just turned six. A few years later she also lost her father and her younger brother. Betty became a communicant at the Reformed Episcopal Church of the Atonement in Germantown, where Bishop William Culbertson, later president of Moody Bible Institute in Chicago, was her rector.

A friend invited Betty to hear Dr Robert C. McQuilkin, Bible teacher and Presbyterian pastor, speak at a conference centre in New Jersey. 'I made major life decisions each day of that week under his ministry,' Betty said. The last evening the conference guests gathered for Communion following the missionary hour, at which Dr McQuilkin had said that there were 500 million people who had never once heard the name of Jesus. After the bread had been passed for the Lord's Supper, Dr McQuilkin asked, 'Has anyone been overlooked in the passing of the bread?' 'All I could think of were 500 million hands being raised everywhere,' Betty said. 'I asked the Lord to let me go as a missionary to people who had never heard the name Jesus.'

Betty decided to study at Columbia Bible College, where Dr McQuilkin, the school's founder, taught the Bible. She graduated, and stayed on for eleven years as McQuilkin's secretary, but in her heart Betty still felt that she was called to be a pioneer missionary. At the Bible College, Betty met Mary Beam. They discovered that they shared a call to missions somewhere in Africa. Mary applied to the Sudan Interior Mission and was sent to Ethiopia in 1935. She had to leave the country in 1938, when Ethiopia was occupied by Italians who had entered World War II on the side of Germany.

Forced out of Ethiopia, the Sudan Interior Mission began work in neighbouring Anglo-Egyptian Sudan, where Mary was assigned to the Mabaan tribe. After a year's furlough, she returned to Africa in 1941 aboard the old Egyptian liner *Zam Zam*. The ship left New York on March 19 bound for South Africa, with several hundred passengers, many of them missionaries. On April 17 the *Zam Zam* was shelled and sunk by a Nazi warship. Intent on helping others, Mary was one of the last to leave the ship—even after the captain and crew! When a damaged and overcrowded lifeboat began to take on water, Mary gave her place to a mother and her six children. Mary jumped into the shark-infested ocean singing 'Jesus Never Fails.'

Mary and the other passengers were rescued by a German commercial ship that was closely following the warship. There were 322 refugees on a ship fitted out to carry 28 passengers and the crew. The Germans carefully avoided the British blockade and, after thirty-three danger-ous days of travel, they reached occupied France. Since the United States had not yet entered the war, the Americans were allowed to go home. Mary said, 'I learned many things, especially about the presence of God at all times. At every crisis—there were at least six—we sighted a rainbow, the biblical sign of promise. This gave us courage.'

The *Greenville Piedmont* gave front-page coverage on June 30, 1941, to Mary's story, reporting that three months after the *Zam Zam* was sunk Miss Beam 'was back after travelling 18,000 miles without getting anywhere near her destination.' She was staying with her parents in Greenville, the journalist explained, 'until she can again start for her mission post, which she plans to do "as soon as possible."' Moving to Columbia, Mary joined Betty Cridland and a small group of women living in an apartment near Columbia Bible College. For a few months she taught missions at the college and visited churches to talk about her experiences in Africa. Betty, whose plans to go to Africa had been frustrated by her failure to pass the required medical exams, finally got a better report and was accepted by the Sudan Interior Mission. Mary Beam and Betty Cridland travelled together to Africa in 1942, arriving after seventy-seven days at sea on an Egyptian ship that took its time to avoid German submarines.

The two women were sent to different mission stations, but Mary was reassigned to work with Betty among the Uduk people in the Blue Nile Province, located uneasily between the northern and southern regions of the Sudan, in the borderland close to the Ethiopian frontier. In 1938 the Sudan Interior Mission had secured a foothold at Chali, in the heart of Uduk country, when Malcolm and Enid Forsberg, formerly serving in Ethiopia, moved there.[2] Christian missions were not allowed by the government to locate in the more central and and important parts of Southern Sudan, but were permitted to work in what were regarded as particularly primitive and difficult areas. At Chali the Forsbergs gradually built up a core of people who were open to their gospel message. Interrupted by Italian military action in the area during 1940, the SIM was able to take up its work at Chali again in 1941.

In 1943 Mary Beam and Betty Cridland joined the Forsbergs at Chali. Malcolm Forsberg wrote:

> We had met Mary only once in Ethiopia, then again, briefly, in the Sudan, where she had gone directly from Ethiopia. She was a hard worker and never spared herself. Her lean, freckled face was surmounted by a tangle of red hair. When Mary was in a hurry, which was most of the time, her hair had to hang on as best it could. It received little attention from Mary. Betty had been carefully brought up in one of Philadelphia's better suburbs and had grown up in the Episcopal Church on *The Book of Common Prayer*. She was about five feet two, was well built, and her dark hair was rarely out of place. She hurried through her many tasks and knew how to break up an hour into twenty-minute periods that could be used to finish three jobs. Mary and Betty had met at Columbia Bible College. It was there that the Christ of the prayerbook came alive for Betty. When Mary returned to the Sudan she brought Betty with her. They complemented each other. Betty was the student and linguist. Mary eventually handled the workmen, the car, travel equipment, and helped in school discipline and boarding matters.[3]

Betty described their early missionary days at Chali:

> At night we heard mosquitoes trying to get through the screen of net and also the weird prowling noises of

the lions, leopards, hyenas, roaming through the tall grass often very close to our screened sleeping porch. We were sometimes awakened by animal horns being blown ferociously, some to the left of our compound, some to the right. We knew that it was a summons to tribal war to begin at dawn. That summons never went unheeded by anyone—never, until God's Spirit through his Word worked in the lives of Uduks making them new creatures in Christ Jesus, eager and willing to be warriors for Christ.

Malcolm Forsberg wrote about the mission at Chali, 'This is man's work. But the Lord has given strength and determination to these two young ladies, and they have carried on right through the mud, mosquitoes, and real dangers.' Under 'Miss Beam and Miss Betty,' as they came to be known affectionately by all, a substantial church community was built up among the Uduks. Others came to help. At one point there were five missionaries at Chali, all women. After mission work in other areas of the Sudan, Barbara Harper served in Chali from 1954 to 1964. Even when Mary and Betty were alone at Chali, when they were 'a team of two, they were not a team of two,' Betty wrote, because God had raised up 'such prayer warriors for us, who prayed us through everything.' Mary and Betty sent regular prayer letters to their supporters at home, full of news about what was going on in and around Chali. They closed each letter with the words 'in the heart of the tall grass' and signed 'Mary and Betty.' People keenly awaited these letters, shared them with their friends, and kept on praying.

Mary and Betty established a lasting friendship with Dr Wendy James, who visited the Sudan frequently and wrote numerous articles and three scholarly books about the Uduks.[4] Despite some major points of disagreement, Mary and Betty appreciated and loved Wendy James, and she loved them. In their Christmas letter for 1992, Betty wrote that 'through the years Dr Wendy James has proven to be a real friend.' James described Mary and Betty as 'missionaries of outstanding ability and personal dedication.'[5] Dr James was critical of the Sudan Interior Mission's 'fundamentalist' legalism and its 'literal' interpretation of the Bible. She had a more positive attitude toward the traditional practices, myths, and culture of the Uduks than did the missionaries. James, who admitted that she was 'not a practicing Christian,' stated: 'I should make it very clear that I am not a complete cynic. I have the utmost respect for those of the Christian community who had rooted their own lives in its teachings, and been touched to the heart, or [as the Uduks] would say, liver, by the love of Jesus and the power of the God of the Bible.'[6]

Many were sceptical that two or three women missionaries could do anything to change the Uduks. The British District Commissioner for the Blue Nile Province said to Betty, 'Miss Cridland, would you tell me what brought you to this place?' Betty answered, 'Well, Mr Long, I believe God sent me here.' He answered, 'If you think you can do anything with the Uduks more power to you.' What Betty thought was 'yes, we've got all the power of God'! Psychologists from the University of Heidelberg visited Chali a number of times. They told Mary and Betty that they had not found a people who had been so taken up with fear as the Uduks. The Heidelberg scholars could scarcely believe the change they now found. Betty wrote that she and Mary were able to share with 'these wonderful psychologists what the power by which God raised the Lord Jesus Christ was able to do' in the lives of this primitive people. In 1983 an older Uduk Christian said, 'From long ago people were always being killed because of fear of evil spirits. This has ceased now. Because Jesus is very big. People get to know Jesus and leave this behind.'

From the very beginning of their work, the missionaries tried to convince the Uduks to abandon their practice of killing twins. Twins were considered a curse and were buried alive, and their mothers were feared and despised. All babies whose mothers died in childbirth were buried in a grave with their mothers. As they put the living child on top of its mother in the grave, the witch doctors shouted, 'Follow your mother! She's lost, and you're lost too.'

In 1952 an Uduk woman named Doatgay arrived at the Forsbergs' home with her recently born twins. She told the missionaries, 'My people said I couldn't stay in the village with the curse on me, so I came to you.' Mona, the first Christian convert among the Uduks, who lived with the Forsbergs, said to her: 'You don't have to be afraid of the old talk anymore, Doatgay. The paper [the Uduk word for the Bible] tells us that twins too are people. We who believe the paper are not afraid of twins. God will help you and we will help you.' 'What have you named the babies?' Enid Forsberg asked. 'Twins in our tribe have never lived long enough to have names. You name them,' Doatgay replied. Enid said, 'The Lord has heard us in this matter of twins. We'll call them Borgay and Thoiya—Praise and Prayer.'[7] They were the first Uduk twins allowed to live, but it would be some time before the tragic custom of killing twins and the babies whose mothers died in childbirth completely ceased.

Mary and Betty began a boarding school at Chali. They spent days getting the consent of parents for boys and girls to come to the school. They found clothes for every child who joined them at the school, bought big pans for cooking food, and hired village women as cooks. They also began to reach out beyond Chali to distant Uduk villages. The two women started out on ten-day evangelistic trips, travelling by foot and donkey. They returned dishevelled, tired, and caked with mud from head to foot, but remained only long enough to pick up clean clothes before trekking out to another section of the tribe, bringing to more and more people the good news of the Christian message.

The church at Chali was organized on June 1, 1949. There were nine members. Two were chosen to be elders. Mary suggested that the little church should be called 'Chali Inter-tribe Church' because its people came from three different tribes. 'This is the Lord's doing, and it is wonderful in our eyes,' said Mary. The two elders conducted the church's first Communion service. It brought great joy to the missionaries to receive Communion for the first time from the hands of Uduk elders.

One of the most important events in the story of the Chali mission was the conversion of an intelligent and gifted young man named Rasha Angwo. When Mary and Betty first saw Rasha, he was standing beside his chief in the position of repose that Uduk men take, the right foot on the left knee, balancing easily on one foot. He had a glistening spear and his throwing stick in his right hand. He was covered with the red oily mixture that the Uduks used for dress. He had a waistband of beads and iron bracelets wound tightly around his arms. Rasha struggled between the new Christian faith and his revered tribal customs, but slowly became convinced that God's way was best. In the church at Chali, Rasha stood and said, 'All these years I have refused God and His Word to me, but now I stand to say that I want to be for God with one liver [one heart] and one stomach [Uduks think and act with their stomachs] only for Him and I want him to take possession of me and I want to be all for Him.'[8]

Rasha Angwo became an effective teacher of the Men's Bible Class, explaining Christian teaching in a way that men could understand:

> Men, you know that when we really love to swim, as you and I do, we don't stay in the shallow places. We get out into the deep water. The Apostle Paul was like that in the Word of God. Oh, men, I want to be like Paul. I want to go and sound the depths of the Word of God. As I have been studying this to teach you, Satan has tried to suffocate me, as he tried to suffocate Paul. And men, I want to tell you, come on out and swim where the water is wonderful. You have the Holy Spirit to help you when Satan tries to cut off your breath.

Rasha married Susgay. When they had twins, Susgay, who was not yet a Christian, was in agony because she knew that she would be a disgrace to her family if she did not kill her babies. Rasha sat by her side—an Uduk had never done such a thing—and said over and over, 'Susgay, I love you. I don't refuse you. I love the boys. They're our sons. We want them, Susgay. I'll help you.' Rasha and Susgay were the first Uduks to raise their own twins. Susgay became a Christian and was baptized in June 1956.

With the training Mary and Betty had given him, Rasha was ordained as the first pastor of the church at Chali.[9] He received a new name—'Pastor Paul,' after his favourite Bible figure. In addition to Uduk and English, he also spoke Arabic, the trade language in Southern Sudan. From the early days of the mission, Bible translation was an important part of the missionaries' work. The Forsbergs had made a beginning, and Mary and Betty, with Barbara Harper, carried on with 'heroic perseverance,' said Wendy James.[10] Pastor Paul assisted the missionaries in their translation work. He could always, it seemed, find the right Uduk word to express what the Bible was saying.

Mary and Betty's 1957 Christmas letter reviewed what had been achieved at the mission. The boys' school, founded in 1948, had sixty pupils, and the girls' school, founded two years later, had fifty. An orphanage was dedicated in 1956 to care for the ten orphan children who had been living in missionaries' homes, including three sets of twins who had been rescued. The Chali church, organized in 1949, had a pastor, seven elders, eighty-eight baptized believers, representing five tribes, and a Sunday congregation of two to three hundred. It was the centre for a network of smaller outlying churches. There were ninety-nine adults in reading classes, the Uduk dictionary had been produced by Mary and Betty,[11] and several sections of the New Testament had been translated.

Chali was considered part of Southern Sudan until 1953, when the Uduk area was returned to the North. The mission at Chali was allowed to continue its work, although now within the boundaries of a northern province. Violence, instigated by Muslim soldiers, broke out. The church at Chali with its 'lovely new thatched roof' was burned.[12] Government restrictions on missions and missionaries increased with intensification of civil war. Malcolm Forsberg's *Last Days on the Nile* describes the growing opposition to Christian missions. By the end of 1963 most of the missionaries in Southern Sudan had left or been deported. Christmas of 1963 was the last that Mary and Betty had with their people and the church at Chali. In the Christmas service, attended by Muslims as well as Christians, the story of Jesus' birth in Luke was read in thirteen different languages. The church provided food for all—thin pancakes and hot meat sauce.

Several weeks later the first two copies of the American Bible Society's Uduk *New Testament* was delivered by a Missionary Aviation Fellowship plane, to the great joy of missionaries and people.[13] Pastor Paul wanted to do something special for the dedication of the Uduk *New Testament*. He had one of the boys in the school draw a picture of Satan and put it on a baobob tree, believed by the Uduks to be the special location of evil spirits in the village. On the picture were written words from 2 Corinthians 4:4—'The god of this world has blinded the minds of the unbelieving so that they could not see the light of the gospel of the glory of Christ.' A great crowd, from the outlying villages as well as from Chali, gathered to watch as men from the oldest to the youngest came with shining spears and took turns throwing their spears into the picture of Satan on the tree. Then followed a service of celebration in the church.

Mary, Betty, and Barbara Harper were deported with a few days' notice in April 1964. The people came with tears, gifts, and, best of all, with words of faith and comfort: 'The Lord Jesus you brought to us will not leave with you. He will always stand with us and strengthen us to live for Him at any cost until we with Him meet you when He comes. And you have left us the New Testament in our very own hands to feed us and to guide and keep us true to Him through His Holy Spirit.' Amazingly, a full shipment of the Uduk New Testament arrived a few days before the missionaries had to leave. Mary and Betty gathered all the empty dried-milk cans they had stored and filled them with New Testaments, hymn books, primers, notebooks, and pencils. They gave these to the Christians who could read (Mary and Betty had by then trained about a thousand Uduks to read) with the request that they read the New Testament in their villages every night and teach others to read.

On the missionaries' last day the church was filled. The Chali congregation sang in Arabic and several tribal languages a favourite song:

> I have decided to follow Jesus,
> No turning back, no turning back.
> The cross before me, the world behind me,
> No turning back, no turning back.

Armed police urged the missionaries to get moving. Pastor Paul told the functionaries, 'We always pray when people start on their journey.' The police stepped back while the pastor lifted his voice in thanksgiving for the missionaries who had come to bring them the good news and had stayed to teach them about it. He also prayed for members of the government and for the police by name that they might come to know the Lord! The missionaries were then led away from their beloved home in the heart of the tall grass. 'Heartbroken, numb, bewildered,' Mary and Betty and their people believed even so that God makes no mistakes. 'This was not something over which God had no control,' they said. Pastor Paul sent a message for American Christians:

> For so many years our African peoples, and especially we in the Sudan, lived in darkness and blindness until His faithful pioneer missionaries came to give us the message of deliverance from fear of the evil eye and all the fears too many to mention. Pray for the church of the Sudan at this most difficult time for the Christians, many of whom are so fearful of what is going to take place after the departure of the missionaries. Pray for the church of the Sudan that it may be a strong uncompromising church no matter what the price. Pray for the pastors of the Sudan that they may not fall into any snares and be led astray. Pray that all of us Sudanese Christians may always be true to our Lord Jesus Christ and depend wholly on Him in every time of need, knowing that Jesus will build His church and the gates of hell will not prevail against it.

Three weeks after the missionaries left, the Christians gathered in the church for a Bible study heard a great noise. They rushed outside and found that the baobob tree had fallen! The Christians celebrated, saying, 'The pastor told us the truth. He told us that the true Spirit now dwelled in us, and that we need not fear the evil spirits any longer. The evil spirit tree has crashed.'

After deportation from the Sudan, Mary Beam and Betty Cridland went as missionaries to Somalia, but after six months the Muslim Brotherhood forced their departure from that country. They then moved to Kenya, where they served under the Africa Inland Mission, teaching Bible on the tea plantations in the highlands. The Kenya Church, the first church on the tea plantations, with the Chali Church in the Sudan, were, Betty said, 'our beloved "plantings of the Lord."' The work of Mary and Betty in Kenya ended when they were advised to leave because of serious medical problems. They returned to the United States but did not retire. They served for ten years with the Bible Alliance in Florida producing and distributing cassettes of the Bible in over twenty languages.[14] Pastor Paul came to the United States in 1981 to read aloud the whole New Testament in Uduk for sets of 24 cassettes. Moving to Greenville, South Carolina, Mary's hometown, Mary and Betty became ministers-at-large for the Africa Inland Mission. They carefully followed the developments at Chali and the Uduk dispersion to Ethiopia and other places. This news they shared with their many friends in church mission conferences and through their greatly loved prayer letters.

In Chali Pastor Paul and the elders carried on during a difficult time. Dr Wendy James wrote:

> I had heard of Pastor Paul some time before I ever arrived in Chali. He and the Chali Church were well known in the Blue Nile Province in the 1960s ... As a Christian outpost, right on the border with the

rebellious South, Chali had already acquired some notoriety. Pulling the Church through the civil war period, when outside financial aid and other help was reduced to an intermittent trickle, was a real achievement on Paul's part, and required a political tightrope act of no little skill ... He was able to sow the seeds of the extraordinary Christian revival which began in 1967 and to keep it going ... Pastor Paul now presides, almost elder-statesman-like, over a much expanded network of Church groups ... He is regarded by most outsiders as a spokesman for all the Uduk. Paul has little in the way of conventional education, but his fluent English (slightly Southern-states American, and slightly biblical) gives no hint of this; his cheerful and easy social manner makes any visitor feel welcome.[15]

When Wendy James visited Chali in December 1967, she found that astonishing changes had taken place. She wrote, 'There had been a sudden, and to me quite unexpected, expansion of Christian activity, not only in Chali but in the surrounding countryside. I heard from Pastor Paul himself that 523 people had been baptized in a single day [in November] and that many more were being prepared.' The younger people were forsaking old tribal customs and taking up hymn-singing, Bible classes, and team games. The church in Chali and the smaller outlying churches were overflowing each Sunday. On December 17 a second mass baptism was held, which Dr James attended. She wrote, 'From the church we went in a very long procession to the river, and in groups of seven, Paul baptized the new believers. I counted 186.' Betty said that when she and Mary prayed for revival, 'little did we realize that part of the cost of the revival we were praying for would be the forced departure of the missionaries.'

Whatever material benefits may have attracted Uduks to Christianity in the earlier period, and these were fairly limited, were not a factor in the later revivals. 'The new Christianity must rely on faith alone,' wrote Dr James. She added, 'There is perhaps a general prestige in joining the church, at a time when the presence of Islam is increasingly conspicuous, but this circumstance aside, it is the figure of the dead and risen Christ which touches the thought and feeling of the Uduk in a way for which Islam, for example, can offer no parallel.'[16]

At the end of the first civil war in 1972, Chali was once more accessible. In December, Mary and Betty made a two-day visit, the first missionary faces seen in Southern Sudan after the expulsion. They felt, they said, that they had 'touched the edges of heaven.' People embraced them, showed them twins who had been saved, told them about those who had died 'in Jesus,' and thanked them for the Bibles that had been left in their hands.

In 1987 Sudan's Muslim government overran villages in the South, killing many people, and destroying homes and crops. Nineteen Uduk churches were burned, including the church at Chali, killing an elder and his wife who were inside. When the ashes from the burning church were taken by the wind into the clouds, the people watching believed that they saw two faces. 'Oh, look,' they said, 'Our first two martyrs are being received by Jesus in heaven.' Some 20,000 Uduk-speaking people were scattered, mostly to Ethiopia, but also to Northern Sudan, Kenya, Uganda, and to the

United States, Canada, and Australia. 'The [Uduk] community was by now as good as 100 per cent acknowledged Christians,' Wendy James wrote.[17]

Dr James visited the Uduks in several camps. These people who 'have experienced some of the grossest indignities and sufferings known to mankind,' she wrote, had the reputation of being 'model refugees' because of 'their desire not to receive emergency relief more than to get themselves established.' They were known for their 'hard work, and their being a happy people, in spite of suffering and persecution as they made at least five border crossings because of bombings, looting, factions, ethnic persecution.'[18]

Pastor Paul found himself stranded in Khartoum at the time of the devastation of his church and surrounding villages in 1987. Together with some church elders he had gone north for a conference, and could not safely return. Martin Luther, an elder still in Chali, became a pastor. Like his namesake, he stood firm, Betty wrote in one of her letters 'like the Rock of Gibraltar.' In 1991 Martin Luther spoke with Dr James after a Sunday service in the open air in Ethiopia. She taped his message to the Sudan Interior Church people in Khartoum, asking them to write to Miss Beam and Miss Betty in the United States. He firmly stated that 'we shall not leave Arumgimis [the Uduk word for the biblical God, meaning 'the Spirit above']. He is with us here in the bush.'[19]

Betty wrote in their June 1992 prayer letter that 'our Pastor Paul, for whom so many have prayed, went to be with the Lord on March 11.' There were memorial services for Pastor Paul in Khartoum and across the refugee camps in Uduk churches in Ethiopia. As the churches gathered to remember their beloved pastor, there was a prayer, a hymn such as 'Faith is the Victory that Overcomes the World', scripture reading, and a sermon. In one of these services a Uduk pastor said: 'We are here to remember our father, Pastor Paul. We have lost him but he is in the hand of God. He is not lost to human beings. All the churches are in his hands. They were all his. He was like a centre pole for us, the church started with him and has branches which have now spread out. We came today to honour him and give his soul to God.'[20] Dr James sent Mary and Betty cassette recordings of three of the memorial services for Pastor Paul. For many years Pastor Paul had prayed that his son, Nathan Paul, could go to Columbia Bible College where Miss Beam and Miss Betty had studied. When Nathan Paul received his master of divinity degree at the college, Betty was present to witness the graduation of the son of the first Uduk pastor in Southern Sudan.

In November 1993 Mary and Betty visited the large Uduk refugee camp in Ethiopia, along with Dr John Oliver (pastor of the First Presbyterian Church in Augusta, Georgia), Mrs Oliver, and some of the people from their church.[21] Over 10,000 Uduks gathered for the conference, listening to Dr Oliver preach on the Good Shepherd's Love, the Water of Life, and the Bread of Heaven. Betty spoke in the Uduk language from the book of Daniel about how Daniel served God in exile. One day a huge crowd of people shared in a feast of three bulls and other food provided by the Georgia church.[22]

The Uduk church in Ethiopia continued to grow. Dr James witnessed a mass baptism in 1994. She wrote:

At least 500 people assembled a mile upstream on the banks of the Baro river for a ceremony of baptism. I believe there had been others but this was the largest since their arrival, and was carried out in great style by Pastor Joshua Hashu and attendants. Several dozen people, not only youngsters but adult men and women, were baptized in batches, as Joshua preached about John the Baptist in the wilderness of Judea, wearing sackcloth and living on locusts and honey, [and] calling all the people of Israel to God.[23]

In one of her last prayer letters Betty wrote: 'Not all missionaries have the great joy of living to see the results of God's working in the lives of those to whom they were privileged to bring the gospel of the Lord Jesus Christ. But Mary and I continually give thanks for how God is causing the Uduks to witness in so many different areas of the world now. Uduk churches are functioning in all places where Uduks are now living.'[24]

Shirley Duncan, long-time member of Greenville's Second Presbyterian Church, said, 'How we loved Mary and Betty. Those dear ladies attended our church in their later years and were such a blessing to us.' Paige McCarty, a close young friend who helped care for Mary and Betty during their last years, said, 'They were loving and giving and interested and active in missions and people until they left for heaven.'

On her ninety-fourth birthday, Betty wrote: 'Mary joins me in sending much love to all of you. We do have wonderful times of prayer each day and Mary reads the Bible to me since I can no longer read it for myself. She also reads *Daily Light*, the devotional book we have used all our lives together.'

Mary Beam died on April 5, 2002, and Betty Cridland exactly nine months later. Both funeral services, identical except for the hymns, were held at Mitchell Road Presbyterian Church in Greenville and conducted by John Oliver, their Augusta pastor, and Robert Richardson, long-time friend and generous supporter, who played second base for the New York Yankees from 1955 to 1966. The closing hymn in Mary's service was 'Jesus Never Fails,' the song she had sung as she jumped into the sea at the sinking of the *Zam Zam*.

Anthony Ogala Osimbo, who came from Kenya to study at Columbia Bible College, said:

> If God hadn't used Mary and Betty to lead my parents to Christ, then I wouldn't be here. I'm really thankful that they obeyed the Lord to go to Africa, despite all that they had to go through while they were there. I thank Him so much ... Whoever I lead to Christ and however many, it will always trace back to how the Lord touched Mary and Betty ... like multiplication.[25]

How beautiful are the feet of those
who preach the good news!

A PRAYER

Heavenly Father!
Send the good news of your salvation
to the ends of the earth.

Be with your missionary servants
who are engaged in preaching the gospel.

'Take their feet, and let them be
Swift and beautiful for thee;
Take their lips and let them be,
Filled with messages from thee.'

Turn the hearts of many people to Christ,
and make them obedient to your truth.

Amen.

ENDNOTES

Chapter 1: John Eliot

Ola Elizabeth Winslow, John Eliot: 'Apostle to the Indians'
(Boston: Houghton Mifflin Company, 1968), 96, 100. Recent
studies of John Eliot are Richard W. Cogley, *John Eliot's Mission
to the Indians before King Philip's War* (Cambridge: Harvard
University Press, 1999); and Kathryn N. Gray, *John Eliot and
the Praying Indians of Massachusetts Bay: Communities and
Connections in Puritan New England* (Lewisburg: Bucknell
University Press, 2013). Cogley and Gray provide helpful information about Eliot's life, but the best source is still the book
by Ola Winslow. Following the title page of her book is a
quotation from Richard Baxter: 'The world is better able to read
the nature of religion in a man's life than in the Bible.' Winslow
begins her book with the sentence, 'Among the stalwart ones of
New England's first generation, John Eliot holds his place in the
small group of men who wrote their names indelibly on the first
pages of our national history.'

[2] A memorial window to John Eliot was placed in the Church of St.
John the Baptist, Widford, by his American descendants in 1894.
A telegram was sent by Eliot's Roxbury church in Massachusetts
with the words, 'We honour the memory of our Apostle and try
to carry on his work.'

[3] Winslow, *John Eliot*, 9, 16, 20.

[4] From Holland, Hooker emigrated to Massachusetts, and became pastor of the church at Newtown (Cambridge) in 1634. Pastor and congregation moved to Connecticut in 1636. *The New International Dictionary of the Christian Church* states that Hooker was 'the founder of Connecticut' and 'perhaps the most powerful pulpit orator of his day.' He died in 1647.

[5] Cogley, *John Eliot's Mission to the Indians*, 45.

[6] Winslow, *John Eliot*, 29.

[7] Winslow, *John Eliot*, 35, 39, 120.

[8] A member of Boston's first church, Anne Hutchinson began to question the doctrine of most of the colony's ministers. She attracted many to her way of thinking who went so far as to interrupt church meetings with their protests. Winslow writes that Hutchinson demanded independence for herself, but 'was also the assailant of those who believed differently' (63). A civil and a church trial banished Hutchinson from the colony and excommunicated her from the church. She had sealed her fate in claiming that God supernaturally and directly communicated his will to her. She went to Rhode Island and later to Long Island Sound, where she was killed by Indians in 1643.

[9] There is no completely satisfactory way to refer to the American Indians. 'Native Americans,' 'natives,' and 'Indians' are all used interchangeably.

[10] Andrew F. Walls, 'Missions and Historical Memory: Jonathan Edwards and David Brainerd,' in *Jonathan Edwards at Home and Abroad*, edited by David W. Kling and Douglas A. Sweeney (Columbia, SC: University of South Carolina Press, 2003), 252.

[11] Winslow, *John Eliot*, 105, 106, 107.

[12] Winslow, *John Eliot*, 100.

[13] Cogley, *John Eliot's Mission to the Indians*, 72, 125.

[14] Gray, *John Eliot*, xv.

[15] Winslow, *John Eliot*, 132-33.

[16] Cogley, *John Eliot's Mission to the Indians*, 169.

[17] The Society for the Propagation of the Gospel was the first Protestant missionary society and continued its support of missions to the North American Indians for more than three centuries.

[18] Cogley, *John Eliot's Mission to the Indians*, 112.

[19] Cogley, *John Eliot's Mission to the Indians*, 138.

[20] Winslow, *John Eliot*, 144.

[21] Cogley, *John Eliot's Mission to the Indians*, 119.

[22] Winslow, *John Eliot*, 95.

[23] Gray, *John Eliot*, 139.

[24] Gray, *John Eliot*, p. 141. Gray commented in 2013 that 'in its most recent incarnation, Eliot's language primer is appropriated to meet the political and cultural needs of present-day Natick descendants. We are delighted to find this small tribe of Native Americans still practicing the blend of Puritan and traditional teachings that their forefathers and John Eliot evolved 350 years ago' (147).

[25] Gray, *John Eliot*, 134.

[26] Cogley, *John Eliot's Mission to the Indians*, 4-5.

[27] Cogley, *John Eliot's Mission to the Indians*, 165.

[28] Winslow, *John Eliot*, 162-63.

[29] Winslow, *John Eliot*, 165-66.

[30] *The New International Dictionary of the Christian Church*, 338.

[31] Cogley, *John Eliot's Mission to the Indians*, 148.

[32] Deer Island is now a peninsula in the Boston Harbor since the channel separating the island from the mainland was filled in by the 1938 hurricane.

[33] Winslow, *John Eliot*, 174.

[34] Winslow, *John Eliot*, 175-76.

[35] Winslow, *John Eliot*, 177.

[36] Gray, *John Eliot*, 114.

[37] Winslow, *John Eliot*, 179.

[38] Winslow, *John Eliot*, 181, 183.

[39] Cogley, *John Eliot's Mission to the Indians*, 247.

[40] Winslow, *John Eliot*, 184.

[41] John Eliot Jr was probably the only Massachusetts Bay Puritan besides his father who learned the Algonquian dialect well enough to preach in it. Eliot's son-in-law, Habbakuk Glover, preached in English to the ever-growing native population who had learned English. Timothy Woodbridge, a great-grandson of John Eliot, went as schoolmaster for the mission to the Mahican Indians in western Massachusetts in 1734. Jonathan Edwards joined this mission after his dismissal by the church at Northampton.

[42] Cogley, *John Eliot*, 46.

[43] Winslow, *John Eliot*, 3.

[44] Winslow, *John Eliot*, 185, 191.

Chapter 2: David Brainerd

[1] There have been many editions of Brainerd's diary and journal. They are included in The Banner of Truth Trust publication of *The Works of Jonathan Edwards* (1974), and referenced in these endnotes as *Works of Jonathan Edwards* (Banner of Truth). *The Life of David Brainerd*, edited by Norman Pettit, appeared in 1985, as volume 7 in *The Works of Jonathan Edwards*, published by Yale University Press, and referenced in the endnotes as *Works of Jonathan Edwards* (Yale). A convenient source for Brainerd's diary and journal, edited by Philip E. Howard, was published by Moody Press in 1949. This book integrated Brainerd's diary and journal, but summarized or omitted Edwards's editorial comments as well as his lengthy conclusion, which was Edwards's valuable 'Reflections and Observations on the Preceding Memoirs of Mr Brainerd.' Howard's goal was to make 'available again a fairly complete record of the self-denying life and strenuous labors of David Brainerd as he preached the gospel to the American Indians.' Howard's book went through a number of printings. In 1989, rights to the volume were acquired by Baker Books, which issued its seventeenth printing in 2007. I would have preferred to use only the Banner of Truth or the Yale sources, but my aging eyes required the larger and clearer print of the Moody volume. It is referenced in the endnotes as *Life of Brainerd* (Moody). For a recent and very important book about Brainerd, see *The Lives of David Brainerd: the making of an American Icon* by John A. Grigg (Oxford University Press, 2009).

[2] Grigg, *The Lives of David Brainerd*, 25.

[3] *Life of Brainerd* (Moody), 59.

[4] *Life of Brainerd* (Moody), 59-69. Grigg, *The Lives of David Brainerd*, 10-12.

[5] Iain H. Murray, *Jonathan Edwards: A New Biography* (Banner of Truth Trust, 1987), 301.

[6] Grigg, *The Lives of David Brainerd*, 38. The only surviving Brainerd sermon (located at the Yale Divinity School Library) is in Grigg's opinion Brainerd's licensing sermon.

[7] Grigg, *The Lives of David Brainerd*, 38.

[8] Brainerd did not use the word 'heathen' in a racial or demeaning sense. He also refers to 'white heathen.' *Life of Brainerd* (Moody), 222. Andrew Walls writes that for Brainerd 'heathenism was not a religion but a state of mind, and it had nothing to do with race.' Andrew F. Walls, 'Missions and Historical Memory: Jonathan Edwards and David Brainerd,' in *Jonathan Edwards at Home and Abroad*, edited by David W. Kling and Douglas A. Sweeney (Columbia, SC: University of South Carolina Press, 2003), 257.

[9] *Life of Brainerd* (Moody), 268.

[10] Grigg, *The Lives of David Brainerd*, 53.

[11] Grigg, *The Lives of David Brainerd*, 63.

[12] *Life of Brainerd* (Moody), 383.

[13] *Life of Brainerd* (Moody), 132.

[14] *Life of Brainerd* (Moody), 135.

[15] *Life of Brainerd* (Moody), 154.

[16] Grigg, *The Lives of David Brainerd*, 73.

[17] Walls, *Jonathan Edwards at Home and Abroad*, 258.

[18] *Works of Jonathan Edwards* (Yale), 7:329-30.

[19] *Life of Brainerd* (Moody), 206.

[20] *Life of Brainerd* (Moody). 186-87.

[21] Grigg, *The Lives of David Brainerd*, 83, 115.

[22] *Life of Brainerd* (Moody), 212.

[23] Marsden, *Jonathan Edwards*, 393.

[24] Grigg, *The Lives of David Brainerd*, 91.

[25] In John Grigg's view, 'Brainerd's impact' on Edwards's preaching to the Indians seems clear. Grigg, *The Lives of David Brainerd*, 145.

[26] Marsden, *Jonathan Edwards*, 394.

[27] Michael D. McMullen, ed., *The Blessing of God: Previously Unpublished Sermons of Jonathan Edwards* (Broadman and Holman Publishers, 2003), 246.

[28] *Life of Brainerd* (Moody), 257.

[29] *Life of Brainerd* (Moody), 294.

[30] Murray, *Jonathan Edwards*, 302.

[31] Grigg, *The Writings of David Brainerd*, 98-99.

[32] The town welcome sign in present-day Cranbury, New Jersey, includes the words, 'Here David Branierd, Missionary, Laboured with the Indians.'

[33] *Life of Brainerd* (Moody), 336. Brainerd's work at Cranberry was continued by his younger brother John, who had graduated from Yale in 1746. The flourishing Indian town, called Bethel, was closed when New Jersey officials were able to confiscate the land and forced the departure of the Indians. Some stayed in New Jersey and others moved west to the Susquehanna. In 1834 the Methodist Missionary Herald told about two elderly Indian sisters who lived in Kansas. They traced their spiritual heritage to their grandmother who was one of Brainerd's New Jersey converts. According to the two sisters, their grandmother remembered Brainerd as a 'lovely young man' who 'went about from house to house to talk about religion.' Grigg, *The Lives of David Brainerd*, 123.

[34] In October Dickinson died suddenly, and the college was moved to the care of Aaron Burr in Newark. Burr was said to have remarked that 'if it had not been for the treatment received by Mr Brainerd at Yale, New Jersey College [Princeton] would never have been erected.'

[35] *Life of Brainerd* (Banner of Truth), 2:378.

[36] *Life of Brainerd* (Banner of Truth), 2:33.

[37] Murray, *Jonathan Edwards*, 304.

[38] *Life of Brainerd* (Moody), 170-71.

[39] Grigg writes that 'to ruin this moment of romance,' David went on to tell her that 'he was willing to part with his dear brother John, 'although I love him the best of any creature living.' Grigg, *The Lives of David Brainerd*, 126. Marsden believes that Jerusha, who was 'of much the same spirit with Mr Brainerd,' would have understood and agreed with the 'kingdom priorities' of his comment. Marsden, *Jonathan Edwards*, 326.

[40] Murray, *Jonathan Edwards*, 305.

[41] Grigg, *The Lives of David Brainerd*, 125.

[42] Grigg, *The Lives of David Brainerd*, 135. On Sunday, February 14, 1747, a few months after David Brainerd died, Jerusha died. Her grief-stricken father, preached her funeral sermon, the most personal of all Edwards's sermons, on the poignant words from Job, 'Youth is Like a Flower That Is Cut Down.' Jerusha was seventeen years old, and was, Edwards said, 'generally esteemed the flower of the family.' She was 'remarkably weaned' from the world, 'very indifferent about all things whatsoever of a worldly nature, setting her heart' on another world. She 'declared in words, showed in deeds' that she was 'ever more ready to deny herself, earnestly inquiring in every affair which way she could glorify God.' Edwards had Jerusha's body buried next to David Brainerd's in the Northampton Cemetery. He was, writes Marsden, 'confident that their souls were already blissfully

united in Christ, yet in what seems for him an unusual display of earthly sentiment, he placed her remains next to Brainerd's, awaiting the bodily resurrection.' Marsden, *Jonathan Edwards*, 328.

[43] *Life of Brainerd* (Banner of Truth), 2:315.

[44] Grigg, *The Lives of David Brainerd*, 136.

[45] Marcus L. Loane, *They Were Pilgrims* (Banner of Truth Trust, 2006), 33.

[46] *Life of Brainerd* (Moody), 46.

[47] *Life of Brainerd* (Moody), 111-12.

[48] *Life of Brainerd* (Moody), 119.

[49] *Life of Brainerd* (Moody), 188-89.

[50] *Life of Brainerd* (Moody), 50.

[51] *Life of Brainerd* (Moody), 130.

[52] *Life of Brainerd* (Moody), 174.

[53] *Life of Brainerd* (Moody), 181.

[54] *Life of Brainerd* (Moody), 198.

[55] *Life of Brainerd* (Moody), 365.

[56] *Biographical Dictionary of Evangelicals*, 205.

[57] *Life of Brainerd* (Moody), 51.

[58] Marsden, *Jonathan Edwards*, 331.

[59] Marsden, *Jonathan Edwards*, 331.

[60] The following quotations are found in *Life of Brainerd* (Moody) on pages 75, 86, 95, 99, 116, 127, 140, 150, 159, 166, 197-98, and 353.

[61] Marilynne Robinson, *New York Times* Book Review, September 24, 2017, 13.

[62] John Piper, *The Hidden Smile of God: the fruit of affliction in the lives of John Bunyan, William Cowper, and David Brainerd* (Crossway Books, 2001), 158.

Chapter 3: John Leighton Wilson

[1] Hampden C. DuBose, *Memoirs of Rev. John Leighton Wilson. D.D., Missionary to Africa and Secretary of Foreign Missions* (Richmond, Va.: Presbyterian Committee of Publication, 1895), 116.

[2] Henry H. Bucher, Jr., 'John Leighton Wilson and the Mpongwe: The "Spirit of 1776" in Mid-Nineteenth Century Western Africa,' *The Journal of Presbyterian History* (Fall 1976), 291, 309.

[3] Wilson's middle name, 'Leighton,' was probably in honour of the Scottish minister Robert Leighton, who was principal of the University of Edinburgh from 1653 to 1662. Despite his Presbyterian connections and views, Leighton agreed with hesitation to accept appointment as Archbishop of Glasgow in 1670, hoping to bring about some degree of conciliation between Episcopalians and Presbyterians. His commentary on 1 Peter was published a few years after his death in 1684 and has rarely been out of print since. The Leighton Library in Dunblane contains a collection of Robert Leighton's books, some 1,400 volumes in all, some in Greek, Persian, Syrian, and Gaelic. It is the oldest private library in Scotland.

[4] John Miller Wells, *Southern Presbyterian Worthies* (Richmond, Va.: Presbyterian Committee of Publication, 1936), 50, 28

[5] Wells, *Southern Presbyterian Worthies*, 50-51, 29

[6] *Memorial Volume of the Semi-Centennial of the Theological Seminary at Columbia, South Carolina* (Columbia, S.C.: Presbyterian Publishing House, 1884), 1666.

[7] John Leighton Wilson, *Western Africa: Its History, Condition, and Prospects* (London: J. Wilson, 1850), 518. Wilson's book was reprinted by Harper & Brothers (New York) in 1856 and 1969.

In 1970 it was reprinted again by the Negro University Press in Westport, Connecticut.

[8] Robinson, *Columbia Theological Seminary*, 110.

[9] DuBose, *Wilson*, 56

[10] *Memorial Volume*, 405

[11] DuBose, *Wilson*, 42.

[12] DuBose, *Wilson*, 47.

[13] DuBose, *Wilson*, 54.

[14] DuBose, *Wilson*, 212.

[15] DuBose, *Wilson*, 71.

[16] Bucher, 'John Leighton Wilson,' 295.

[17] Bucher, 'John Leighton Wilson,' 295.

[18] DuBose, *Wilson*, 190.

[19] Bucher, 'John Leighton Wilson,' 309.

[20] Bucher, 'John Leighton Wilson,' 295.

[21] Bucher, 'John Leighton Wilson,' 294.

[22] Bucher, 'John Leighton Wilson,' 295.

[23] J. Leighton Wilson, *The British Squadron on the Coast of Africa* (London, 1851), 24.

[24] Wilson, *Western Africa*, 526.

[25] Wilson, *The Agency Devolving on White Men in Connection with Missions to Western Africa*, 509.

[26] DuBose, *Wilson*, 212-13.

[27] DuBose, *Wilson*, 218

[28] Bucher, 'John Leighton Wilson,' 301.

[29] DuBose, *Wilson*, 226.

[30] Wilson, *The Agency Devolving on White Men in Connection with Missions to Western Africa*, 524.

[31] DuBose, *Wilson*, 100.

[32] DuBose, *Wilson*, 100

[33] Writing about B. B. Warfield, Bradley J. Gundlach describes 'the dilemma of the antislavery slaveholder—feeling it wicked to hold people in bondage, but wicked too to release them unprepared into a society unprepared to receive them fairly.' Bradley J. Gundlach, '"Wicked Caste": Warfield, Biblical Authority, and Jim Crow,' in *B. B. Warfield: Essays on His Life and Thought* (Phillipsburg, N.J.: P&R Publishing, 2007), 143.

[34] DuBose, *Wilson*, 99.

[35] DuBose, *Wilson*, 238.

[36] DuBose, *Wilson*, 278.

[37] *Southern Presbyterian Journal, October (1859).*

[38] *Southern Presbyterian Review, Vol. 2, No. 3, December 1849*, 430-31.

[39] DuBose, *Wilson*, 247

[40] DuBose, *Wilson*, 243

[41] Ernest Trice Thompson, *Presbyterians in the South* (Richmond, Va.: John Knox Press, 1973) 2:22.

[42] Wells, *Southern Presbyterian Worthies*, 156. 169

[43] Henry Alexander White, *Southern Presbyterian Leaders: 1683–1911* (Edinburgh: Banner of Truth Trust, 2000), 405.

[44] White, *Southern Presbyterian Leaders*, 343, 199

[45] DuBose, *Wilson*, 104-5.

[46] Thompson, *Presbyterians in the South*, 2:292.

[47] Thompson, *Presbyterians in the South*, 2:94.

[48] *Southern Presbyterian Review, Vol. 2, No. 3, December 1849*, 439, 441.

[49] White, *Southern Presbyterian Leaders*, 406.

[50] William Childs Robinson, *Columbia Theological Seminary and the Southern Presbyterian Church: A Study in Church History, Presbyterian Polity, Missionary Enterprise, and Religious Thought* (Decatur, Ga.; Dennis Lindsey Printing Company, 1931), 138.

[51] Thompson, *Presbyterians in the South*, 2:292.

[52] Thompson, *Presbyterians in the South*, 2:292.

[53] Thompson, *Presbyterians in the South*, 3:122.

[54] White, *Southern Presbyterian Leaders*, 408.

Chapter 4: David Livingstone

[1] Andrew Ross, *David Livingstone: Mission and Empire* (Hambledon and London, 2002), 2. There are over one hundred biographies of David Livingstone. The earliest books pictured him as a servant of God who became a great missionary and courageous champion of Africans, giving his last years and ebbing strength to fighting the slave trade. Florence Nightingale called him 'the greatest man of his generation' (Jeal, *Livingstone*, 1). Stephen Neill wrote, 'I have not found it necessary to revise my opinion, formed many years ago, that the two great men of the nineteenth century were Abraham Lincoln and David Livingstone' (Stephen Neill, *Churchman 93 [1] 1979, 75*). Later studies often concentrated on Livingstone's faults and failures and his supporting role in the European colonization of Africa. Tim Jeal's *Livingstone*, published in 1973, the year of the centenary of Livingstone's death, 'seemed intended to reduce Livingstone to a good deal less than half-size,' wrote Stephen Neill. Julie Davidson believes that despite Jeal's sharp criticism of Livingstone, he has 'no doubt that Livingstone's vision and achievements made him a great man' (*Looking for Mrs Livingstone*, Edinburgh: St Andrew Press, 2012, xix). While sharply critical of Livingstone at some points, Cecil Northcott in *David Livingstone: His Triumph, Decline and Fall* (Philadelphia: Westminster Press, 1973), states that his 'critical judgment is in no sense a demolition. [Livingstone] remains essentially, I think, a great and unique person.' 'If I have laid the accent on failure,' Northcott writes, 'it is because somewhere within that failure lies the essence of his triumph' (9). In a review of Oliver Ransford's *David Livingstone: The Dark Interior* Stephen Neill wrote: 'Dr Ransford ... shows us plainly [the] less pleasant side [of David Livingstone]; but he never loses sight of the real greatness of the man—his love for Africa and Africans, his

deep hatred of the slave trade, his concern for the spread of the gospel, the immense services he rendered to Africa.' The best book about David Livingstone is, in my opinion, by Andrew Ross, Honorary Fellow of the Faculty of Divinity, University of Edinburgh. He avoids the extremes of hagiography and defamation that characterize so many treatments of Livingstone.

2 Ross, *Livingstone*, 2.

3 Ross, *Livingstone*, 4.

4 Northcott, *Livingstone*, 20.

5 Ross, *Livingstone*, 10.

6 Ross, *Livingstone*, 17.

7 See 'Robert Moffat "Africanus"' by Iain H. Murray in his *A Scottish Christian Heritage* (Edinburgh: Banner of Truth Trust, 2006), 241-74. Murray quotes J. Du Plessis who wrote in his classic *History of Christian Missions in South Africa*, 'Robert Moffat was undeniably the greatest missionary which [the London Missionary Society] sent to South Africa—the greatest in natural ability, in patient devotion to duty, and in deep, transparent piety' (243-44).

8 Northcott, *Livingstone*, 22.

9 Ross, *Livingstone*, 23.

10 Ross, *Livingstone*, 38-39.

11 Northcott, *Livingstone*, 14.

12 For a much-needed book about Mary Moffat Livingstone, see Julie Davidson, *Looking for Mrs Livingstone*. Alexander McCall Smith writes in the introduction that Davidson 'has created in this remarkable work of historical and geographical reflection a fascinating picture of a remarkable life.' Julie Davidson, although 'not a practicing Christian,' is generally quite respectful of religion. When an African Christian shares with

her the story of his life, with its trials and difficulties, and states, 'It is in God's hands,' she was tempted to disagree but writes that she has 'too much respect for the faith that sustains so many struggling people in Africa' (70). Davidson describes herself as 'an agnostic.' At times she allows her personal opinions to influence or even shape her interpretation of events and issues in the lives of Mary and David Livingstone. She is too quick to offer what she believes the Livingstones and others were thinking or what they might have said. She acknowledges that she made deductions about Mary's 'state of mind which can't be verified by her own testimony' (243). Even so, Julie Davidson has added a valuable resource for the study of Mary Livingstone and her husband.

[13] Ross, *Livingstone*, 41, 50.

[14] Ross, *Livingstone*, 60.

[15] Ross, *Livingstone*, 65.

[16] Ross, *Livingstone*, 84.

[17] Davidson, *Looking for Mrs Livingstone*, 226.

[18] Davidson, *Looking for Mrs Livingstone*, xxi.

[19] Davidson, *Loooking for Mrs Livingstone*, 69.

[20] Ross, *Livingstone*, 107. 'A hundred thousand welcomes,' with which every verse of the poem begins, is a translation of the traditional Gaelic welcome.

[21] Ross, *Livingstone*, 115.

[22] William Monk, ed., *Dr Livingstone's Cambridge Lectures* (Cambridge: Deighton, Bell & Co., 1860), 168.

[23] Ross, *Livingstone*, 132.

[24] Northcott, *Livingstone*, 85.

[25] Julie Davidson, *Looking for Mrs Livingstone*, 220.

[26] Ross, *Livingstone*, 203.

[27] Northcott, *Livingstone*, 37.

[28] Ross, *Livingstone*, 219.

[29] H. M. Stanley, *How I Found Livingstone* (London, 1872), 410-11.

[30] Ross, *Livingstone*, 230.

[31] Ross, *Livingstone*, 232.

[32] Ross, *Livingstone*, 230.

[33] Ross, *Livingstone*, 235.

[34] *Scottish Life*, 15.

[35] See Northcott's chapter seven, 'Sizing up the Doctor,' 89-105.

[36] Northcott, *Livingstone*, 31.

[37] Northcott, *Livingstone*, 14.

[38] Northcott, *Livingstone*, 68.

[39] Ross, *Livingstone*, 52.

[40] Ross, *Livingstone*, 210.

[41] Davidson, *Looking for Mrs Livingstone*, 45.

[42] Ross, *Livingstone*, 56.

[43] Ross, *Livingstone*, 96.

[44] Davidson, *Looking for Mrs Livingstone*, xix.

[45] Jeal, *Livingstone*, 1, 384.

[46] Philip Jenkins, *The New Faces of Christianity: Believing the Bible in the Global South* (Oxford: Oxford University Press, 2006), 9.

[47] Davidson, *Looking for Mrs Livingstone*, 171, 175.

[48] Davidson, *Looking for Mrs Livingstone*, 176-77.

49 Northcott, *Livingstone*, 32.

50 Andrew F. Walls, 'David Livingstone 1813–1873: Awakening the Western World to Africa,' in *Mission Legacies: Biographical Studies of the Modern Missionary Movement*, edited by Gerald H. Anderson, Robert T. Coote, Norman A. Horner, James M. Phillips (Marynoll, New York: Orbis Books), 146.

51 *Scottish Life, Spring 2013*, 73.

52 Ross, *Livingstone*, 44.

53 Davidson, *Looking for Mrs Livingstone*, 212.

54 See *The Spiritual in the Secular: Missionaries and Knowledge about Africa*, edited by Patrick Harries and David Maxwell (Grand Rapids: Wm. B. Eerdmans Pub. Co., 2012), 49-51.

55 Northcott, *Livingstone*, 13-14.

56 Walls, 'David Livingstone 1813-1873: Awakening of the Western World to Africa', 146.

57 Jim Gilchrist, 'Dr Livingstone, I Presume,' in *Scottish Life, Spring 2013*, 39-43, 73.

58 Northcott, *Livingstone*, 122.

59 Northcott, *Livingstone*, 129.

Chapter 5: Mary Slessor

[1] Elizabeth Robertson, *The Barefoot Missionary* (Edinburgh: National Museums of Scotland, 2001), 108.

[2] There are scores of books, many for children and teenagers, telling the story of Mary Slessor, and a number of biographies, beginning with W. P. Livingstone's *Mary Slessor of Calabar: Pioneer Missionary* (London: Hodder & Stoughton, 1915). James Buchan's *The Expendable Mary Slessor* (Edinburgh: Saint Andrew Press and New York: The Seabury Press) was published in 1980 and 1981. Elizabeth Robertson's *Mary Slessor: The Barefoot Missionary* (Edinburgh: National Museums of Scotland) appeared in 2001. Jeanette Hardage's *Mary Slessor—Everybody's Mother: The Era and Impact of a Victorian Missionary* (Eugene, Oregon: Wipf & Stock) came out in 2008. David Clyde Jones writes that this book is 'an undertaking of immense scholarship and understanding likely never to be surpassed' (*Presbyterion: Covenant Seminary Review*, 41/1-2, 62). In the introduction Hardage writes, 'I was drawn to Mary Slessor because of her faith, her certainty that she was where God wanted her to be, her desire to go and teach and be a witness of the good news a people had not yet heard' (xii). A recent book *Lives of Scottish Women: Women and Scottish Society, 1800-1980* by William W. J. Knox (Edinburgh: Edinburgh University Press, 2006) includes a chapter on 'Mary Mitchell Slessor: Serving God and Country' (117-39). Knox presents Mary Slessor as a dedicated servant of God and a supporter of the British program of colonization. He recognizes, however, the ambiguous nature of his evidence for the latter point. A better title for this writing would be: 'Mary Slessor: Serving God and the Africans.'

[3] Robertson, 6.

[4] Thomas Cheyne and Samuel Driver were Old Testament scholars who promoted German higher criticism in England and Scotland.

[5] Hardage, 221.

[6] Robertson, 9.

[7] Buchan, 25.

[8] Hardage, 150-51.

[9] Hardage, 151.

[10] Hardage, 34. Statues of Mary Slessor depict her holding a twin in each arm.

[11] Robertson, 94.

[12] Buchan, 229.

[13] Hardage, 25-26.

[14] Quoted by Iain H. Murray in his *A Scottish Christian Heritage* (Banner of Truth Trust, 2006), 216.

[15] Hardage, 222.

[16] Buchan, 71.

[17] Hardage, 150-51.

[18] Hardage, 208. The two remaining copies of Slessor's Bible are in the McManus Galleries and Museum in Dundee.

[19] Hardage, 221.

[20] Livingstone, 45.

[21] Livingstone, 51.

[22] Hardage, 212.

[23] Hardage, 60.

[24] Livingstone, 319.

[25] Buchan, 184, 196.

[26] Hardage, 112.

[27] Robertson, 65.

[28] Hardage, 106.

[29] Buchan, 137.

[30] Buchan, 111.

[31] Hardage, 202.

[32] Hardage, 201-202.

[33] Hardage, 211.

[34] Buchan, 79.

[35] Hardage, 213.

[36] Hardage, 214.

[37] Hardage, 189.

[38] Hardage, 224.

[39] Buchan, 247.

[40] Hardage, 231.

[41] Hardage, 187.

[42] Hardage, 188.

[43] Hardage, 238.

[44] Hardage, 238.

[45] *Presbyterion: Covenant Seminary Review*, 41/1-2, 62.

[46] Hardage, 209.

[47] Livingstone, 212.

[48] Hardage, 231.

[49] Buchan, 180.

[50] Livingstone, p. 20.

[51] Hardage, 226.

[52] Hardage, 228.

[53] Livingstone, 175.

[54] Buchan, 200.

[55] Hardage, 256.

[56] Buchan, 224.

[57] Robertson, 103.

[58] Buchan, 230-31.

[59] Buchan, 232-33.

[60] Robertson, 104.

[61] Hardage, 231.

[62] Robertson, 105.

[63] Buchan, 243.

[64] Buchan, 187.

Chapter 6: Samuel Norvell Lapsley

[1] Lapsley, *Life and Letters*, 39. See endnote 3.

[2] Robert Benedetto, 'The Presbyterian Mission Press in Central Africa, 1890-1922,' *American Presbyterians, 68.1 (Spring 1990)*, 55.

[3] James W. Lapsley, ed., *Life and Letters of Samuel Norvell Lapsley: Missionary to the Congo Valley West Africa, 1866-1892* (Richmond, Virginia: Whittet & Shepperson, 1893) and *William Henry Sheppard, Presbyterian Pioneers in Congo* (Richmond, Virginia: Presbyterian Committee of Publication) are primary sources for the lives of Lapsley and Sheppard. William Sheppard dedicated his book 'To THE SOUTHERN PRESBYTERIAN CHURCH which took me as a half-clad, barefoot boy and trained me for the ministry of Christ, and to which I owe all I am or ever hope to be.' Lapsley's Life and Letters and Sheppard's Presbyterian Pioneers are included in *Four Presbyterian Pioneers in Congo* (published by First Presbyterian Church in Anniston, Alabama, in 1965, in observance of the 100th anniversary of the birth of Samuel Lapsley). See chapter 7, endnote 2.

[4] Lapsley, *Life and Letters*, 19.

[5] Sheppard, *Presbyterian Pioneers*, 15.

[6] Sheppard, *Presbyterian Pioneers*, 17.

[7] Sheppard, *Presbyterian Pioneers*, 17.

[8] Sheppard, *Presbyterian Pioneers*, 19.

[9] Lapsley, *Life and Letters*, 26.

[10] Lapsley, *Life and Letters*, 40.

[11] Lapsley, *Life and Letters*, 49.

[12] Lapsley, *Life and Letters*, 43-44.

[13] Lapsley, *Life and Letters*, 44.

[14] Lapsley, *Life and Letters*, 49.

[15] In 1899 Joseph Conrad published *Heart of Darkness*, revealing in fiction the truth of the exploitation of the Africans by European traders like 'Mr Kurtz,' who had a 'heart of immense darkness.'

[16] Lapsley, *Life and Letters*, 52.

[17] Sheppard, *Presbyterian Pioneers*, 30.

[18] Lapsley, *Life and Letters*, 66.

[19] Sheppard, *Presbyterian Pioneers*, 30.

[20] Lapsley, *Life and Letters*, 71.

[21] Lapsley, *Life and Letters*, 88.

[22] Lapsley, *Life and Letters*, 89.

[23] Sheppard, *Presbyterian Pioneers*, 63.

[24] Sheppard, *Presbyterian Pioneers*, 36.

[25] Sheppard, *Presbyterian Pioneers*, 39.

[26] Lapsley, *Life and Letters*, 132.

[27] Lapsley, *Life and Letters*, 200.

[28] Lapsley, *Life and Letters*, 94.

[29] Lapsley, *Life and Letters*, 83.

[30] Sheppard, *Presbyterian Pioneers*, 84.

[31] Lapsley, *Life and Letters*, 137. This is the second verse of 'In Heavenly Love Abiding,' words by Anna Waring, music by Mendelssohn.

[32] Lapsley, *Life and Letters*, 110.

[33] Sheppard, *Presbyterian Pioneers*, 62.

[34] Sheppard, *Presbyterian Pioneers*, 94.

[35] William E. Phipps, *William Sheppard: Congo's African American Livingstone* (Louisville: Geneva Press, 2002), 60.

[36] Lapsley, *Life and Letters*, 208.

[37] Sheppard, *Presbyterian Pioneers*, 64.

[38] Lapsley, *Life and Letters*, 201.

[39] Sheppard, *Presbyterian Pioneers*, 137.

[40] Sheppard, *Presbyterian Pioneers*, 132.

[41] Sheppard, *Presbyterian Pioneers*, 132.

[42] Lapsley, *Life and Letters*, 206.

[43] Lapsley, *Life and Letters*, 197.

[44] Phipps, *William Sheppard*, 46.

[45] Lapsley, *Life and Letters*, 201.

[46] *Four Presbyterian Pioneers*, 56, 109.

[47] Lapsley, *Life and Letters*, 231.

[48] Lapsley, *Life and Letters*, 230-31. *The Biographical Dictionary of Christian Missions* sums up Samuel Lapsley's short missionary career. He began the analysis and study of several languages of the Kasai area of the Congo, 'recorded native songs and customs, initiated the translation of hymns and portions of the Bible,' and, with his colleague, 'launched the organization of a strong indigenous church.' *Biographical Dictionary of Christian Missions*, ed. Gerald H. Anderson (New York: Simon & Schuster Macmillan, 1998), 383.

[49] Sheppard, *Presbyterian Pioneers*, 65.

[50] Sheppard, *Life and Letters*, 85-86.

⁵¹ *Four Presbyterian Pioneers*, 124.

⁵² *Gospel Hymns*, No. 2, 31. Words by Jane Crewdson, music by Ira D. Sankey. Forty-four years before Samuel Lapsley died, John Leighton Wilson wrote some words that apply to that young missionary whom Wilson would have loved. 'If the career of many of those servants of Christ who went to [Africa] was short, the fruits of their labours were most abundant, and eternity may disclose that they lived to greater purpose than thousands who have been spared to reach the ordinary term of human life. "That life is long which answers life's great end"' (Wilson, 'The Agency Devolving on White Men in Connection with Missions to Western Africa,' 519).

⁵³ Sheppard, *Presbyterian Pioneers*, 56.

Chapter 7: William Henry Sheppard and Lucy Gantt Sheppard

[1] Kennedy, *Black Livingstone*, vii. See endnote 2.

[2] William Henry Sheppard described his early years in Africa in *Presbyterian Pioneers in Congo* (Richmond: Presbyterian Committee of Publication, 1917). Dr. S. H. Chester wrote in the introduction to Sheppard's book, 'The reader will be struck with the way in which, in telling his story up to the time of Mr. Lapsley's death, he always keeps Mr. Lapsley to the front and himself in the background ... The characteristic modesty of Dr. Sheppard should not be permitted to deprive him of the honour which justly belongs to him as one of the two pioneers and founders of this mission, which has developed into one of the most interesting and successful missions to be found anywhere in the world.' *Four Presbyterian Pioneers in Congo* was published by First Presbyterian Church in Anniston, Alabama, in 1965, in observance of the 100th anniversary of the birth of Samuel Lapsley. Included in this book are four publications: *Life and Letters of Samuel Norvell Lapsley* edited by James W. Lapsley; *Presbyterian Pioneers in Congo* by William H. Sheppard; *Maria Fearing: A Mother to African Girls* by Althea Brown Fearing; and *Lucy Gantt Sheppard: Shepherdess of His Sheep on Two Continents* by Julia Lake Kellersberger. Two biographies of Sheppard were published in 2002—William E. Phipps, *William Sheppard: Congo's African American Livingstone* (Louisville: Geneva Press), and Pagan Kennedy, *Black Livingstone: A True Tale of Adventure in the Nineteenth-Century Congo* (New York: Viking Penguin). Kennedy's lively book reads like a novel, but suffers from overuse of imagination and personal bias. Kennedy admits creating 'a kind of speculative biography' in her depiction of Lucy Sheppard. She does the same thing with

William Sheppard. She has little use for what she calls 'professional religionists' and tries to separate Sheppard as far as she can from them. The result is a distortion of that missionary's convictions and accomplishments. Phipps's book, while less exciting to read, is more balanced and accurate, not so much 'a true tale' as a careful history.

³ Sheppard, *Presbyterian Pioneers*, 100-101.

⁴ Sheppard, *Presbyterian Pioneers*, 107-108.

⁵ Sheppard, *Presbyterian Pioneers*, 108.

⁶ Walter L. Williams, *Black Americans and the Evangelization of Africa, 1877-1900* (Madison, WI: University of Wisconsin Press, 1982), 25. In *Black Americans and the Evangelization of Africa, 1877-1900*, Walter L. Williams writes, 'Sheppard, because of his influence on black Americans and his efforts on behalf of Africans, deserves to be ranked among the most important of early Afro-American missionaries.'

⁷ For Lucy Gantt Sheppard's life, see Julia Lake Kellersberger, *Lucy Gantt Sheppard: Shepherdess of His Sheep on Two Continents* (Atlanta: Committee on Woman's Work, Presbyterian Church in the United States, 1938), as well as the books listed in endnote 2.

⁸ *Four Presbyterian Pioneers in Congo*, 5-6.

⁹ *Four Presbyterian Pioneers in Congo*, 7.

¹⁰ *Four Presbyterian Pioneers in Congo*, 9.

¹¹ The Fisk Jubilee Singers, which had disbanded in 1878, was reorganized by Frederick J. Loudin as the Loudin Jubilee Singers.

¹² *Four Presbyterian Pioneers in Congo*, 10.

¹³ *Four Presbyterian Pioneers in Congo*, 14. Miss Fearing spent twenty years in the Congo where she became 'a mother to African girls.' Three of the first converts received into the church

in Luebo were girls under the care of Miss Fearing. She died on May 23, 1937, at the age of ninety-nine.

14 *Four Presbyterian Pioneers in Congo*, 27.

15 *Glorious Living: Informal Sketches of Seven Women Missionaries of the Presbyterian Church, U. S.* (Atlanta: Committee on Woman's Work, 1973) includes chapters on two of the African American women who served as missionaries in Congo: 'Maria Fearing: A Mother to African Girls,' by Althea Brown Edmiston (285-318) and 'Althea Brown Edmiston: A Congo Crusader,' by Robert Dabney Bedinger (260-86). Althea Brown Edmiston joined the Congo Mission in 1902, and 'through scholarship, education, medical treatment and simple kindness, [she] made her presence felt by thousands.' Cary Patrick, 'Althea Brown Edmiston, Giving a Language, Bringing the Word,' in *Go Therefore: 150 Years of Presbyterians in Global Mission*, ed. Cary Patrick (Atlanta: Presbyterian Publishing House, 1987), 63. Before 1937, five black women were assigned to the Presbyterian Congo Mission. They were all born in Alabama and attended Southern black colleges.

16 A year later the Congo mission received another black missionary, Joseph E. Phipps. He had been born and raised in St Kitts in the West Indies and trained in Chicago at Moody Bible Institute. His grandfather was Congolese.

17 *Four Presbyterian Pioneers in Congo*, 11.

18 Phipps, *William Sheppard*, 102.

19 *Four Presbyterian Pioneers in Congo*, 18.

20 Phipps, *William Sheppard*, 105.

21 Sheppard, *Presbyterian Pioneers*, 150-51.

22 *Four Presbyterian Pioneers in Congo*, 24.

23 *Four Presbyterian Pioneers in Congo*, 24.

24 James H. Smylie, 'Sheppard and Morrison, African Mission and Justice,' in *Go Therefore, 150 years of Presbyterians in Global Mission* (Atlanta: Presbyterian Publishing House), 110.

25 Phipps, *William Sheppard*, 120.

26 Phipps, *William Sheppard*, 130.

27 Calence Clendenen, Robert Collins, and Peter Duignan, *Americans in Africa 1865-1900* (Stanford: Hoover Institution, 1966), 63. There are some two million Presbyterians in the Congo, and almost a thousand churches.

28 Kennedy, *Black Livingstone*, 159.

29 *Four Presbyterian Pioneers in Congo*, [11].

30 *Four Presbyterian Pioneers in Congo*, 25.

31 *The Missionary, Sept. 1910*, 450.

32 Phipps, *William Sheppard*, 156.

33 Phipps, *William Sheppard*, 158.

34 Phipps, *William Sheppard*, 165.

35 Phipps, *William Sheppard*, 166.

36 *Four Presbyterian Pioneers in Congo*, 26.

37 Kennedy, *Black Livingstone*, 182.

38 Phipps, *William Sheppard*, 170-71.

39 *Four Presbyterian Pioneers in Congo*, 26.

40 Kennedy, *Black Livingstone*, 186.

41 Arthur Conan Doyle, *The Crime of the Congo* (New York: Doubleday, 1909), iv.

42 Phipps, *William Sheppard*, 178.

43 Named for John Leighton Wilson, missionary to Africa and

major figure in the development of a missionary vision in the
Southern Presbyterian Church.

44 *Four Presbyterian Pioneers in Congo*, 27.

45 Sheppard, *Presbyterian Pioneers*, 151-52.

46 Phipps, *William Sheppard*, 189.

47 Williams, *Black Americans and the Evangelization of Africa,* 25.

48 Kellersberger, *Lucy Gantt Sheppard*, 28.

49 Kellersberger, *Lucy Gantt Sheppard*, 28.

Chapter 8: James A. Bryan

1 The only book about James A. Bryan is *Religion in Shoes: Brother Bryan of Birmingham* by Hunter B. Blakely (Richmond, Virginia: John Knox Press, 1934; revised edition 1953). In these endnotes Blakely's book is referenced by the author's last name. Dr Manford George Gutzke, professor at Columbia Theological Seminary, required his students to read *Religion in Shoes*. One of those students, Kennedy Smartt, wrote, 'Reading that story probably influenced my philosophy of ministry as much as anything I ever read. Because of that I became a pastoral evangelist' (*I Am Reminded*, 14).

2 Blakely, 29.

3 Blakely, 85.

4 Blakely, 21.

5 Third Presbyterian Church, located on the city's Southside at 617 22nd Street South, is affiliated with the Presbyterian Church in America.

6 Blakely, 168.

7 Blakely, 34-35.

8 Blakely, 97.

9 Blakely, 100.

10 Blakely, 39.

11 Blakely, 109-10.

12 Blakely, 68.

13 Blakely, 68.

[14] Blakely, 65.

[15] Blakely, 82.

[16] Blakely, 36.

[17] Blakely, 174.

[18] Blakely, 47.

[19] Blakely, 47-48.

[20] Blakely, 48.

[21] Blakely, 50.

[22] Blakely, 52.

[23] Blakely, 51.

[24] Blakely, 88.

[25] Blakely, 114.

[26] Blakely, 113.

[27] Blakely, 47.

[28] Catherine Marshall, *A Man Called Peter: the story of Peter Marshall* (New York: McGraw-Hill, 1951), 30.

[29] Blakely, 59, 61-62.

[30] Blakely, 91, 127.

[31] Blakely, 30.

[32] Blakely, 81.

[33] Blakely, 91.

[34] Blakely, 88-89.

[35] Blakely, 90.

[36] Blakely, 143-44.

37 Blakely, 146.

38 Blakely, 143-44, 146, 150-51.

39 Blakely, 149.

40 Blakely, 152.

41 Blakely, 160.

42 Blakely, 167.

43 Blakely, 172-74.

44 Blakely, 180.

45 The statue is located at the corner of 11th Avenue and 20th Street.

46 Blakely, 181-82.

47 Blakely, 29.

48 A book of Bryan's sermons was published in Birmingham by A. H. Carter (no date).

49 Blakely, 187.

50 Blakely, 188.

51 Blakely, 62.

Chapter 9: Bob Childress

[1] Richard C. Davids, *The Man Who Moved a Mountain* (Philadelphia: Fortress Press, 1970). This is the only book about Robert W. Childress. The author writes, 'Almost all of this book comes direct from Bob, his wife Lelia and their seven children, his brother Hasten, and from the scores of mountaineers to whom Bob Childress was counsellor, friend, and brother' (xi). There are few other sources for Bob Childress' life and ministry. Two articles about him appeared in *Presbyterian Survey*: 'A Great Work—A Consecrated Worker' by L. H. Patterson (March 1949): 102-04; and 'Preacher Childress Recalls Gun-totin' Days at Church' by Hamilton Crockford (November 1950): 486-87. My thanks to Elder Bill Crisp of Sandhills Presbyterian Church in Southern Pines, North Carolina, who gave me a copy of *The Man Who Moved a Mountain* and thereby introduced me to this remarkable man.

[2] Davids, 17.

[3] Davids, 26.

[4] Davids, 28, 29.

[5] Davids, 30.

[6] Davids, 31.

[7] Davids, 39.

[8] Roy Smith was born in Pelham, South Carolina, in 1888. He studied at Davidson College, Union Theological Seminary in Virginia, and Princeton Theological Seminary. He lived in The Hollow and served in mountain mission work from 1915 to 1925. He later was pastor of churches in Virginia, West Virginia, and Georgia.

[9] Davids, 52, 59.

[10] Davids, 61.

[11] Davids, 70.

[12] Davids, 73.

[13] Davids, 76.

[14] Davids, 59, 81.

[15] Davids, 80, 81, 146.

[16] Davids, 139.

[17] Davids, 178.

[18] Davids, 112.

[19] Davids, 137.

[20] Davids, 114, 140-41.

[21] Davids, 150.

[22] On December 6, 2006, the six Childress rock churches—Buffalo Mountain, Slate Mountain, Bluemont, Mayberry, Dinwiddie, and Willis—were added to the Virginia Landmarks Register. Five are active Presbyterian churches today. Willis is now a Baptist church.

[23] Davids, 154-56, 172.

[24] Davids, 145, 43, 253.

[25] Davids, 218-19. A friend of mine, a non-Christian, wrote to me: 'Thanks again for letting me read your article about the life of Bob Childress. Done. What a classic tale of conversion and dedication, told with warmth and engagement! He must have been quite a gentleman to have had such success among the hardened liquor addicts and knife-toting brigands of the Buffalo. I would have loved to have been a mouse under a leaf, watching him change the minds of his would-be killers, and

then give them all a ride home!'

[26] Davids, 149, 182.

[27] Davids, 244.

[28] Davids, 244-45.

[29] Davids, 238.

[30] Davids, 253.

[31] Davids, 237.

[32] https://mayberrychurch.org/f/docs/bobchildress. html. Bob Childress Jr. served three of his father's churches. His son, Stewart Childress, followed his father and grandfather as pastor of these churches.

[33] Davids, 213.

[34] 'By Faith We See the Hand of God' by Keith Getty, Kristyn Getty, and Stuart Townsend, 2009.

Chapter 10: Mary Beam and Betty Cridland

[1] There are no books telling the remarkable story of Mary Beam and Betty Cridland. Mrs. John Oliver supplied me with many pages of prayer letters, personal letters, and articles about them from her extensive collection. Paige McCarty shared with me information about their last years and the funeral services for Mary and Betty. Quotations without endnotes are all taken from this material.

[2] Malcolm Forsberg, *Land Beyond the Nile* (New York: Harper & Brothers, 1958). Forsberg also wrote *Dry Season: Today's Church Crisis in the Sudan* (New York: Sudan Interior Mission, 1964), *Last Days on the Nile* (Chicago: Moody Press, 1966), and *In Famine He Shall Redeem Thee: Famine Relief and Rehabilitation in Ethiopia* (Sudan Interior Mission, 1975).

[3] Forsberg, *Land Beyond the Nile*, 204.

[4] Dr. James's books are *The Listening Ebony: Moral Knowledge, Religion*, and *Power Among the Uduk of Sudan* (Oxford: Clarendon, Press, 1988); *Kwanim Pa: The Making of the Uduk People* (Oxford: Clarendon Press, 1979); and *War and Survival in Sudan's Frontierlands: Voices from the Blue Nile* (Oxford University Press, 2007).

[5] James, *The Listening Ebony*, 208.

[6] James, *War and Survival*, 251.

[7] Forsberg, *Land Beyond the Nile*, 17-19.

[8] Wendy James wrote, 'This is a powerful image and draws upon deeply rooted understandings of the way in which a spiritual force might seize or enter a person, and change his or her nature.' *The Listening Ebony*, 220.

[9] Paul titled his testimony for his ordination 'The Sad Testimony and Good News to the Uduk tribes.' It is included in Wendy James's *The Listening Ebony*, 346-51. James writes, 'This document eloquently speaks for itself, placing the phenomenon of Christian acceptance in its historical and social context more vividly than I ever could.'

[10] James, *The Listening Ebony*, 219.

[11] Reissued as *Linguistic Monograph Series No. 4 of the Sudan Research Unit of the University of Khartoum* in 1970.

[12] A new church at Chali was built with metal in the late 1970s after two previous buildings were destroyed by fire, set purposely, it was suspected, by Muslims. That church building was destroyed as well.

[13] Pastor Paul had accompanied Betty to the United States, and worked for two months with the linguists at the American Bible Society in New York to prepare for publication the translation of the New Testament in the Uduk language.

[14] The founder and director of the Bible Alliance was Anthony Rossi, an immigrant from Sicily who began and owned Tropicana Orange Juice. For years he was a board member of Columbia Bible College. For his life, see Sanna Barlow Rossi, *Anthony T. Rossi, Christian and entrepreneur: the story of the founder of Tropicana* (Downers Grove, Ill.: InterVarsity Press, 1986).

[15] James, *The Listening Ebony*, 345.

[16] James, *The Listening Ebony*, 252.

[17] James, *War and Survival*, 233.

[18] James, *Kwanim Pa*, 19.

[19] James, *War and Survival*, 251.

[20] James, *War and Survival*, 256.

21 Mary was a member of Augusta's First Presbyterian Church and Betty an associate member. She had continued to be a member of her Episcopal church in Philadelphia since childhood.

22 After a long history as a major church in the Presbyterian Church in the United States (Southern Presbyterian Church) the Augusta church for a few years was independent before joining the Presbyterian Church in America. For many years this church supported and cared for Mary and Betty.

23 James, *War and Survival*, 257.

24 Dr. Wendy James described the Uduk mission under two headings: 'Constructing a Christian community at Chali, 1938-1964' and 'Christianity spreads to the periphery, 1964-1983.' There is now a third heading: Christianity spreads beyond the periphery with the Uduk dispersion.

25 *CIU Connection,* Spring 2003, 10-11.